Q&A

ON THE RCIA

A Guide to Understanding Christian Initiation

Paul Turner

LTP

LITURGY
TRAINING
PUBLICATIONS

Nihil Obstat
Reverend Mister Daniel G. Welter, JD
Chancellor
Archdiocese of Chicago
August 28, 2018

Imprimatur
Very Reverend Ronald A. Hicks
Vicar General
Archdiocese of Chicago
August 28, 2018

The *Nihil Obstat* and *Imprimatur* are declarations that the material is free from doctrinal or moral error, and thus is granted permission to publish in accordance with c. 827. No legal responsibility is assumed by the grant of this permission. No implication is contained herein that those who have granted the *Nihil Obstat* and *Imprimatur* agree with the content, opinions, or statements expressed.

Q&A ON THE RCIA: A GUIDE TO UNDERSTANDING CHRISTIAN INITIATION © 2019 Archdiocese of Chicago: Liturgy Training Publications, 3949 South Racine Avenue, Chicago, IL 60609; 800-933-1800; fax 800-933-7094; email: orders@ltp.org; website: www.LTP.org. All rights reserved. Formerly published as *The Catechumenate Answer Book*.

This book was edited by Timothy A. Johnston. Christian Rocha was the production editor, Juan Alberto Castillo was the designer and production artist.

Cover art by Cody F. Miller. Interior art by Martin Erspamer, OSB.

23 22 21 20 19   1 2 3 4 5

Printed in the United States of America

Library of Congress Control Number: 2018959780

ISBN 978-1-61671-447-5

EQARCIA

AD MEMORIAM

DAVIDIS SCHWARTZE
ÆTERNA CVIVS VITA
RESPONSVM EST VNICVM
QVÆSTIONIBVS OMNIBVS
TERRENA SVPER EIVS VITA

Contents

Acknowledgments xi

Introduction xii

Part 1: Groundwork Questions

What is the catechumenate? 2

What is the RCIA? 2

What are the National Statutes? 4

What are the primary resources for the catechumenate? 5

What is the history of the catechumenate? 5

Why don't we do it the old way, in which the priest did it all? 7

Who should be on a catechumenate team? 7

How does the whole community get involved? 9

How long should the whole process last? 10

Part 2: Precatechumenate

What is evangelization? 12

What is a candidate? 13

What is the difference between a catechumen and a candidate? 14

What is a convert? 15

Which baptisms do we accept? 15

What should we cover in a first conversation? 16

May we accept a candidate from another parish? 17

Do children enter a catechumenate? 18

What is catechetical age? 19

What if the parents, the catechists, or the pastor prefer that children
of catechetical age defer their Confirmation until the children reach the
diocesan age for confirming those young people baptized Catholic
as infants? 20

Can a child be accepted into the catechumenate if the parents
are not interested? 20

What is the precatechumenate or period of evangelization?.................21

What happens at a precatechumenate session?..................................23

Can marital status keep someone from becoming Catholic?.................24

What is an annulment? 25

Part 3: Catechumenate

How do we know when someone is ready to move from
precatechumenate to the catechumenate?...28

What is a sponsor supposed to do? 28

What is the difference between a sponsor and a godparent? 30

What is the Rite of Acceptance into the Order of Catechumens?..........31

What is the Rite of Welcoming? 32

When should the Rites of Acceptance and Welcoming take place? 32

Why does the Rite of Acceptance start at the door of the church? 33

How should the candidates answer the question,
"What do you ask of God's Church?" 34

What is the first acceptance of the Gospel?.......................................36

Why are the candidates signed with a cross?.....................................37

Why does the invitation to the Celebration of the Word of God appear
in the Rite of Acceptance but not in the Rite of Welcoming?................38

Why may catechumens receive a book containing the Gospels
or a cross? 39

Why do we dismiss catechumens at Mass? 41

Should candidates be dismissed at Mass?...42

How does the dismissal happen?...43

What is catechesis?...43

When should catechesis take place?..44

Who leads the catechesis?..45

How does a sample catechetical session look? 46

What are the minor rites?..47

What are Celebrations of the Word?..47

What is an exorcism?..48

Who can lead an exorcism?..49

What are the blessings of the catechumens? 50

When can we use the oil of catechumens? 50

Why does the Period of Purification and Enlightenment coincide
with Lent? 51

Part 4: Purification and Enlightenment

What is conversion? 54

What is discernment?..54

How do you know when someone is ready for Baptism? 55

What issues could keep someone from Baptism?................................56

Under what circumstances does adult initiation happen apart from
Lent and Easter?..58

What is the Rite of Sending? 59

What is the Rite of Election?...59

Why does the Rite of Election take place at the cathedral?.................61

What is the Book of the Elect?..62

Who should sign the Book of the Elect? 62

Should the book be signed at the parish or at the cathedral? 63

May the Rite of Election be repeated? 63

Is the Sacrament of Reconciliation necessary for catechumens
and candidates?...64

What is the Penitential Rite for candidates? 65

What is a scrutiny?..65

Why are the Year A Gospels so important for the scrutinies?.............66

What is a presentation? 67

What is the Presentation of the Creed? 68

What is the Presentation of the Lord's Prayer?...................................69

Should the elect participate in the Triduum? 70

How important are the preparation rites on Holy Saturday? 71

What is the Ephphetha Rite? 71

What is the Recitation of the Creed? 72

Why is there no Recitation of the Lord's Prayer? 73

Should catechumens take a new name at Baptism? 74

What is the paschal fast?....................................75

PART 5: INITIATION

Why does Baptism coincide with Easter?....................................78

Why do we sing the litany of the saints?....................................79

Why is water blessed? 80

Why do the elect make baptismal promises? 80

How do you baptize somebody?....................................81

What is Baptism by immersion?....................................82

Why are the newly baptized not anointed on the crown of the head
with chrism right away? 83

Why do we offer the white garment?....................................85

Why do we give the newly baptized a lighted candle? 86

What is a neophyte? 87

Why do we sprinkle the assembly with holy water at the Easter Vigil?....87

What is the Rite of Reception?....................................89

What if someone from an Eastern Orthodox Church wishes
to become a Catholic? 90

When should the Rite of Reception take place?........................91

When should baptized, uncatechized Catholics receive
Confirmation and First Communion? 92

Why is Confirmation part of the Easter Vigil? 92

Under what circumstances are priests allowed to confirm? 93

Must children of catechetical age baptized at the Easter Vigil also be confirmed?..94

Who should not be confirmed by a priest?.........................95

How is Confirmation administered?...................................96

Why is Communion significant at the Easter Vigil?.............97

How is Communion offered to neophytes?.........................98

PART 6: MYSTAGOGY

What is mystagogy? 100

What does a mystagogy session look like? 101

Why is the Easter octave significant for neophytes?.........102

Why is Year A so important in mystagogy? 103

How do you keep neophytes in mystagogy?.....................103

Why is there a bishop's Mass for neophytes?..................105

What kind of anniversary celebration of Baptism should there be? 105

Should the newly baptized prepare for the Sacrament of Reconciliation? 106

What kind of pastoral care do we offer after mystagogy?..................106

Bibliography 107

Recommended Reading...109

Resources for Group Reflection and Learning 110

I wish to thank

    The North American Forum on the Catechumenate,
    who catechized

    Nick Wagner, who waited

    Mary Ernstmann, Gael Gensler, and Ron Lewinski, who read

    Louis Persac, who baptized

    God, who answers.

                PT

Introduction

If you have questions about the catechumenate, you are in good company. Lots of people do. The catechumenate gives external shape to an interior journey so personal that it raises questions for all who desire to celebrate it with faithfulness and flexibility. If you are helping someone step toward Baptism, Confirmation, and Eucharist, this book is for you.

This book will walk you through a catechumen's journey along the signposts of the RCIA. The RCIA envisions four periods of formation separated by three liturgical steps. Each of these has a unique character, and together they give structure to a process that is ultimately personal and spiritual. Every catechumen's journey from inquiry to Baptism follows a similar path, but each one needs discernment and understanding. The Holy Spirit works in diverse ways to enliven faith in the human heart.

This book will also explore the situation of those with a valid Baptism in another Christian denomination now seeking communion in the Catholic Church. The RCIA calls this group "candidates," and their circumstance differs from the catechumens' because they have already been baptized. In many parishes, ministers and volunteers make little distinction between catechumens and candidates, but baptismal status significantly shapes one's journey toward Eucharistic communion.

Although the revised rites of adult initiation first appeared on the Catholic landscape in 1972, they are still struggling for a stronger foothold in a typical Catholic parish. The RCIA is a large book covering a multitude of circumstances and offering a plethora of options within them. Many people—including many priests—find the book puzzling and challenging.

If you have questions about the catechumenate, you are not alone. You are also in the good company of people from generations long past. In sixth-century Rome, John the Deacon received a list of questions about the catechumenate from Senarius of Ravenna. In the ninth century, Charlemagne sent a series of questions about baptismal rites to the greatest theologians of his day. In the tenth century, the Roman-Germanic Pontifical included a glossary of terms used in the catechumenate for those unfamiliar with them. In the nineteenth century, the question-and-answer format became a popular method of catechesis in works like the *Baltimore Catechism*. Something about the catechumenate just invites questions.

The answers, of course, ultimately lie in the life, ministry, and promise of Jesus of Nazareth. This book hopes to steer you toward the One who pledges salvation, with whom the baptized share the vision of new life.

PART 1:
GROUNDWORK
QUESTIONS

1. What is the catechumenate?

The catechumenate is the preparatory period for adult Baptism. Arranged in stages, it moves people from first faith to full faith as they hear the Word of God and accept the Gospel.

The catechumenate is also the body of people who make this journey of faith. You sometimes hear about someone who is "joining the catechumenate." Such a person is called a catechumen.

You may hear some people mistakenly call catechumens "catechumenates," as in "Our neighbors are catechumenates at St. James." What they mean is "catechumens." The term "catechumen" came into usage in the second century to refer to someone learning about Christianity. It probably carried the idea of God's Word resounding within those who heard it. The word "catechumen" probably shares a root with the word "echo".

"Catechumenate" has yet another meaning. More narrowly, it specifies the period beginning with Acceptance into the Order of Catechumens and ending with Election or the Enrollment of Names. The Church allows people to join the catechumenate at any time of year.

2. What is the RCIA?

RCIA is an acronym for *Rite of Christian Initiation of Adults*. It is the ritual book that details the stages, rites, and processes concerning adult Baptism in the Roman Catholic Church.

The book is one of the fruits of the Second Vatican Council. The council called for a renovation of the Church's liturgy, including the restoration of the catechumenate. Although a complex catechumenate existed in early Christianity, its rites had become rather simplified and its stages eliminated. After the close of the council, study groups implemented the wishes of the world's bishops. One of those groups worked on the catechumenate. The results of their labor were first published in Rome in 1972. A provisional English translation followed in 1974, and the National Conference of Catholic Bishops published the official English translation for the United States of America in 1988. The *Rite of Christian Initiation of Adults* is the Roman Catholic Church's official ritual text for adult Baptism.

Part I describes the procedure for the unbaptized. It divides the process into four stages separated by three rites. The period of evangelization and precatechumenate concludes with the Rite of Acceptance into the Order of Catechumens. The period of the catechumenate concludes with the Rite of Election or Enrollment of Names. The Period of Purification and Enlightenment concludes with the rites of initiation. The period of postbaptismal catechesis or mystagogy comes last.

Part II of the *Rite of Christian Initiation of Adults* contains rites for people in particular circumstances, including children of catechetical age, those in danger of death, and those previously baptized.

The paragraphs throughout the entire book are numbered consecutively. However, the general introduction has its own numeration, causing two sets of paragraphs 1–35. The first appendix continues the main enumeration, but the others have their own numbers. In the right margins throughout, you will find nonconsecutive numbers printed small. These refer to the paragraphs in the 1972 edition in Latin. The 1988 US edition rearranged some of the paragraphs, incorporated material from some other documents, and added some new sections—all with approval by the Apostolic See. You can always tell where the material comes from by checking the right margin.

The book you are now reading will refer you to the ritual text by paragraph numbers, not page numbers. So when you see RCIA, 75, it refers to paragraph 75 of the *Rite of Christian Initiation of Adults*.

Many people use the acronym RCIA to describe a catechumenate group or ministry. ("Join the RCIA!" parishes will promote. Or, "I'm on the RCIA team.") This usage has gained widespread acceptance. However, the acronym does not adequately capture the majesty of the conversion it designates. It also fails to speak to people unfamiliar with its code. Parishes will help the effort if they refrain from using the acronym and substitute more meaningful terms (e.g., "the catechumenate," "Christian initiation," or "becoming Catholic").

More problems have surfaced with the introduction of acronyms based on the acronym. You'll hear about OCIA (the *order* of Christian initiation of adults), RCIC (the rite of Christian initiation of children), and RCIT (the rite of Christian initiation of teens). None of these exist.

"Order" may be a better descriptor than "rite" because the text includes more than ritual rubrics and collects a number of individual "rites." But to fabricate a new acronym dims its value. We have only two official books for Baptism in the Catholic Church. Young children are baptized according to the *Rite of Baptism for Children*. Older children and teens are baptized according to the *Rite of Christian Initiation of Adults*. There is no RCIC or RCIT. Children and teens follow the *Rite of Christian Initiation of Adults*, which includes adaptations for children.

3. What are the *National Statutes*?

The *National Statutes for the Catechumenate* are the local laws governing the catechumenate for the United States, as approved by the National Conference of Catholic Bishops in 1986. They were incorporated into the US edition of the *Rite of Christian Initiation of Adults* and appear in appendix 3. There you can find the specific recommendations that refine the implementation of the catechumenate in the United States.

References in this book to specific numbers of the *National Statutes* will be abbreviated NS.

4. What are the primary resources for the catechumenate?

The main resources are the following:

1. The *Rite of Christian Initiation of Adults* is the basic text. It is the norm according to which other resources are useful.

2. The *Lectionary for Mass* forms the backbone of catechesis throughout the catechumenate. The proclamation of the Word of God is the key to catechetical formation.

3. The *Roman Missal* contains the presider's prayers for many of the rituals. The prayers and prefaces assigned to any given Sunday would also provide material for catechesis.

4. The *Code of Canon Law* contains sections that describe the privileges and responsibilities of catechumens. The most pertinent canons form part of appendix three in the *Rite of Christian Initiation of Adults*. References in this answer book to specific canons will appear in parentheses as follows: (canon 849).

Books and journals flow from many Catholic publishers. These give practical direction for the implementation of the catechumenate. Websites, electronic platforms, and workshops abound to help catechists make better preparations for their ministry.

5. What is the history of the catechumenate?

The catechumenate underwent several different stages in its history. At the time of the apostles, people generally joined the church after a brief experience of catechesis and preaching. In the next few generations, Baptism followed some pattern of formation and sponsorship.

By the fourth and fifth centuries an extended catechumenate had taken shape. People could spend a fairly brief or a considerably longer period as a catechumen before approaching Baptism. Sponsors assisted their preparation. Leaders in the community evaluated their readiness. A series of rituals and periods materialized. Among the sources that describe this period are *The Apostolic Tradition* (3rd to 4th c.), *The Apostolic Constitutions* (3rd to 4th c.), and the writings of Ambrose of Milan (+397), Cyril of Jerusalem (+386), Egeria (late 4th c.), Theodore of Mopsuestia (+428), and Augustine (+430).

By the sixth century, the Christianized world held fewer adult baptisms. The prevailing need for infant baptisms caused some adaptations in the rituals. The catechumenate, once protracted over a period of years, eventually collapsed into a single occasion, celebrated either at the Easter Vigil or in a separate ceremony at any other time of year shortly after an infant's birth.

In the sixteenth century, missionaries could see the value of restoring the catechumenate for their work with unbaptized adults. But they were unable to secure permission from Rome for a catechumenate with rituals in stages.

Permission to redivide the baptismal rite into the stages of a catechumenate finally came in the twentieth century, after centuries of experience with adult Baptism in the missions. The Second Vatican Council restored the catechumenate with mission lands in mind, but its process for initiation proved useful also for countries where the church was well established.

Consequently, although the catechumenate with its odd vocabulary (scrutinies, presentations, catechumen, mystagogy, etc.) looks like something brand-new to many Catholics, its roots go back to the first centuries of our church.

6. Why don't we do it the old way, in which the priest did it all?

Prior to the Second Vatican Council most people joined the Catholic Church by taking "convert instructions," a series of sessions with a priest, extending over a period of several weeks or a few months. During that time, the priest reviewed the basic beliefs of the Catholic Church and invited the persons' assent. He then brought them into the church by Baptism or, if they had already been baptized in some other Christian Church, by conditional Baptism.

Now, however, "the initiation of adults is the responsibility of all the baptized" (RCIA, 9). The entire church hands on and nourishes faith. All in the church—priests, deacons, catechists, parents, godparents, relatives, friends, and neighbors—should take an active part. The involvement of the total community more eloquently expresses what church is all about. Church membership is not just about personal faith worked out with a priest. It means participation in a community of believers.

Preparation this way allows a more relaxed and deeper discernment on the part of the catechumens and of those responsible for their formation. It takes more time. But the involvement of the community is more important than speed.

7. Who should be on a catechumenate team?

Ideally, several people serve on a parish catechumenate team. The makeup of the team will vary from one parish to another depending on resources. Some members may be paid staff (a religious educator, a liturgist, or clergy, for example); others, volunteers (a catechist, sponsor coordinator, or a hospitality minister). When assembling your team, keep in mind some of these responsibilities:

- **Pastoral care.** The catechumenate should assist spiritual growth. Someone or several people on the team—the pastor or spiritual directors—should be watching primarily for signs of faith.

- **Catechesis.** Inquirers will need guidance facing the basic principles of evangelization. Catechumens will need clear formation in the content of faith and the behaviors expected of them. The elect will need spiritual formation. The newly baptized need integration into the community. One or more persons oversee the various catechetical components of the entire process.

- **Worship.** The liturgy of the parish community will invite the catechumens to prayer. Some rituals—like the scrutinies, for example—take place at Sunday Mass. Others—word services, for example—may happen during a separate catechetical session. Whoever oversees parish liturgy will keep other members of the team informed about the various pertinent rituals.

- **Sponsorship.** Everyone becoming a Catholic should have a sponsor or godparent. Someone on the team may recruit, train, and support the volunteers who perform this personal ministry for all who join the church.

- **Children's initiation.** Those skilled in the spiritual growth of children may attend team meetings as well.

- **Discernment.** The entire team shares the critical responsibility to discern the readiness of the individuals at each stage of their preparation toward initiation. Especially before the Rite of Acceptance into the Order of Catechumens and the Rite of Election, they reach a judgment about the progress that the individuals are making.

- **Community involvement.** The team will also help the entire parish community engage in the process of initiation through invitation, example, and prayer.

How you organize the team, how often you meet, and how long people serve are matters you can decide among yourselves as your catechumenate ministry takes shape in the parish.

8. How does the whole community get involved?

Everyone in the Catholic Church shares the responsibility of handing on and nourishing faith. It happens in various ways.

Evangelization. Anyone may meet people who have no church. Catholics can share their faith with acquaintances and invite those seeking to experience more. Some people develop interest in the church after they marry a Catholic spouse. Others take note after involvement in a school or some other outreach of Catholic ministry. We should not simply sit back and wait for people to call us. We need to invite personally and directly.

Catechesis. We all share the responsibility for catechesis as well. Faith formation happens first in homes, especially by parents (*Catechism of the Catholic Church,* 1653, 1656, 2221, 2223). Catechists work with groups of believers. Everyone should consider serving as a sponsor at some time in his or her Catholic life. In casual conversation throughout our day with neighbors, coworkers, and strangers, we have many opportunities to explain what we believe and to display Christian behavior.

Worship. Our faithful attendance at common prayer will engage the whole community in spiritual formation. In private prayer we nurture our relationship with God. On many occasions we pray for catechumens and model our commitment to worship.

Service. By living out our faith in service we give example to the world. Whenever we volunteer our time, our talent, or our treasure, we let catechumens know the full breadth of the Christian life. By personally inviting catechumens to our homes, our meetings, and our service, we integrate them into the Christian family.

Everybody gets involved by doing some things in general and some things in particular. In general, we join as a body of believers to pray and serve. In particular, we use what personal gifts we have to welcome, challenge, and rejoice with catechumens.

9. How long should the whole process last?

As long as it takes. As you'll see, the first two stages are of indeterminate length. Some people may need only a short time in them. Others need more.

The US bishops envisioned that the period of the catechumenate itself would begin before Lent in one year and last until Easter a year later (NS, 6). The RCIA calls it a "gradual process" (4) and says that its length will depend on God's grace, the program, and the human resources on hand to guide (76). This makes it very hard to determine a length of time. Which is good.

This allows a parish to offer individual care to those who are seeking Christ under the guidance of the Holy Spirit. It also provides the necessary space for genuine discernment throughout the process. Sensitive leaders will offer flexible ways that individuals can pursue and deepen their formation, according to the time that best suits their spiritual needs.

PART 2:
PRECATECHUMENATE

10. What is evangelization?

Evangelization is telling people about the Gospel of Jesus Christ. It takes place in many ways.

In the *Rite of Christian Initiation of Adults*, the term has a very narrow usage. It refers to the first period given to unbaptized adults (RCIA, 36–40). During this time we proclaim the basic message of the Gospel to those who express interest in it. The book assumes that the unbaptized have not heard much about Jesus Christ and that the Holy Spirit is prompting their hearts to hear the Gospel for the first time. In pastoral experience, we find that many of the unbaptized know the Gospel fairly well. Although we may proclaim the Good News during this period, it may not come as news to them. On the other hand, the book assumes that those previously baptized who seek to join our church have no need of evangelization, because they have already accepted the Gospel. Pastoral experience shows, however, that some who are baptized do not fully know Jesus Christ.

In other key sources, the term "evangelization" has enjoyed a broader meaning. Pope Paul VI described a "second sphere" of evangelization that reaches out to those who have been baptized but have become indifferent to the faith (*Evangelii nuntiandi*, 56). Pope St. John Paul II lamented the existence of Christian countries where groups of the baptized have lost their faith or no longer consider themselves Christian (*Redemptoris missio*, 33). Citing Pope Benedict XVI, Pope Francis called for an evangelization to "the baptized whose lives do not reflect the demands of Baptism" (*Evangelii gaudium*, 15).

Thus, "evangelization" means bringing the Gospel to people, whether or not they have heard it before. It means letting the Gospel scrutinize the behaviors even of those who have already accepted Christ. Therefore, evangelization also contains a "re-evangelization."

In parishes, evangelization often refers to the outreach we make to people in the community. We extend an invitation to meet Christ at our church. Evangelization in this sense takes many forms: telephone calls, door-to-door visits, community-based ministry, social opportunities— any ministry that specifically invites people to church or opens the door to neighbors who wish to accept some part of the parish's ministry.

Every Catholic shares the responsibility to evangelize. We proclaim the Gospel in word and deed. We invite others to meet Christ through activities at our church.

11. What is a candidate?

The *Rite of Christian Initiation of Adults* uses the term "candidate" in three ways.

1. It refers to an unbaptized person during the period of evangelization (e.g., RCIA, 48).

2. It refers to a baptized Catholic who never received catechesis, Confirmation, or Communion (RCIA, 400).

3. It also refers to those baptized in other ecclesial communities who seek communion in the Catholic Church (RCIA, 400).

You rarely hear the first usage. Before an unbaptized person becomes a catechumen, she or he may be called a candidate. Some people call them "inquirers." This candidate will have a very unofficial relationship with the church and can remain in this stage a long or short period of time.

More frequently, you hear of a "candidate" for Confirmation and Communion in the Catholic Church. The term applies to a person who is already baptized in another church and who is making preparation for these sacraments as a Catholic, but it is also used for baptized but uncatechized Catholics seeking these sacraments.

The US edition of the *Rite of Christian Initiation of Adults* has combined these latter groups of candidates for a significant part of the book. For a clearer reading of these sections (400–504), it is important to know a detail about paragraph 400. The right margin indicates that 400 is a translation of paragraph 295 from the Latin edition with an adaptation inserted for the United States. The insertion is the following phrase from the first sentence: "either as Roman Catholics or as members of another Christian community."

The original intent of 400–410 (295–305 in the Latin edition) was to treat the pastoral care given baptized but uncatechized Roman Catholics. The American edition added to this group those baptized in another Christian community. All the optional rituals that follow (RCIA, 411–472) are creations of the church in the United States for both groups of candidates: those baptized as Catholics and those baptized in other communities. Although these optional rituals for candidates do not appear in the original Latin edition, they are approved by Rome for usage in the United States. However, the Rite of Reception (RCIA, 473–504) specifically pertains to those baptized in other ecclesial communities, not to those baptized as Roman Catholics. Although these distinctions are not evident from a cursory reading of the text, they will influence the proper celebration of sacraments for these groups.

12. What is the difference between a catechumen and a candidate?

Both catechumens and candidates are in preparation for joining the Catholic Church. The main difference is that the catechumen has never been baptized. The main part of the *Rite of Christian Initiation of Adults* concerns catechumens properly called. Most of the processes and rituals for candidates are adaptations.

When assisting a mixed group of catechumens and candidates, it is important that the distinction be made in rituals and terminology. The Baptism that the candidates have already received should always be revered.

13. What is a convert?

A convert is an unbaptized person who becomes a Christian through Baptism. Although people commonly refer to anyone who joins the Catholic Church from another religion as a "convert," the bishops of the United States have asked that the term be reserved to the unbaptized "and never used of those baptized Christians who are received into the full communion of the Catholic church" (NS, 2).

The directive will surprise many Catholics, including some who call themselves "converts", but it comes with a reasonable intent. Catholics share a common Baptism with other Christians, as well as a common membership in a church. A baptized person who joins the Catholic Church is received into the full communion of the church in which he or she already has some standing. A true convert is one who moves from unbelief to Christian belief.

14. Which Baptisms do we accept?

The Catholic Church accepts the validity of a Baptism if the minister intends to baptize and immerses someone in water or pours water over him or her in the name of the Father, Son, and Holy Spirit (canon 849).

Normally a minister who baptizes intends to do this. You usually need not worry about the intent of the minister. The intent is questionable if the minister has a different understanding of the action or words of baptizing.

Both immersion and pouring are acceptable. Sprinkling is not. Note, however, that some ministers in some churches, such as the United Methodist Church, sometimes refer to Baptism by pouring as Baptism by sprinkling. Just because someone uses the term "sprinkling" to describe the method of Baptism does not mean that the Baptism was invalid.

The minister may not use some substance other than water nor attempt to baptize without water at all.

The words for Baptism must be said in the name of the Trinity. ("I baptize you in the name of the Father and of the Son and of the Holy Spirit.") Although some Christian traditions honor Baptism in the name of Jesus alone, the Catholic Church does not.

Consequently, we accept the Baptism of most mainline Christian churches. If a person was baptized in some other way or belonged to a community that did not practice Baptism at all, we regard him or her as unbaptized.

For a current list of valid and invalid baptisms, consult your chancery office. Your diocesan marriage tribunal may also have a local list for the discernment of procedures in annulments. The same list applies to baptized persons interested in becoming Catholic.

Formerly, when someone already baptized wanted to join the Catholic Church we commonly baptized him or her conditionally: "If you are not baptized, I baptize you in the name . . . " Now we are strongly discouraged from following that practice. If a conditional Baptism must take place, it should be done privately, not at the public celebration of the Easter Vigil (NS, 37).

This sensitive issue requires pastoral care. You should not presume a Baptism is invalid unless you have some good reason. A candidate who has already been baptized should not seek Baptism again in the Catholic Church. These restrictions are meant to honor the Sacrament of Baptism and the unity it establishes among Christian churches.

15. What should we cover in a first conversation?

In a first conversation with a potential catechumen or candidate, you want to get some basic information:

- **Who they are.** The usual data—name, address, email, all phone numbers, social media usage, and so on.

- **Where they come from.** Something about their faith story. Their baptismal status.

- **What they believe.** How they began to believe. Their present habits of faith. Their role models. What their tattoos signify.

- **Why they're here.** What made them decide to take this step of their faith journey.

- **Marital status.** Find out if former marriages exist. If there are children.

- **Catholic friends.** It will help to know the names of Catholic friends and family. They may serve as sponsor or godparent down the line.

- **Expectations.** What expectations they have of you. What you expect of them.

16. May we accept a candidate from another parish?

Some people join parishes other than the one in which they live. The same may happen with catechumens and candidates.

Although parish boundaries are permeable, every Catholic parish covers a designated area, and the pastor is responsible for the souls within those geographical boundaries. Therefore, everyone has a Catholic pastor and a parish based on where they live, even if they don't realize it.

If a candidate from outside your parish desires to join the Church, it would be a courtesy to put him or her in touch with the local parish. Catholic parishes usually build their foundational support from people who live in proximity to the church. It enables members to foster strong relationships with the neighbors with whom they bank, shop for groceries, and gas up the car. A Catholic parish generally establishes its primary mission with the community in which it is located. Candidates for initiation will feel more welcome when they meet their neighbors at the church they join. Consequently, you may wish to help candidates from outside your parish make contact with the one in which they live.

However, for various practical and spiritual reasons, parishes may and do accept members from elsewhere.

17. Do children enter a catechumenate?

The *Rite of Christian Initiation of Adults* foresees the need for a children's catechumenate (252–330). An unbaptized child who is no longer an infant should enter a catechumenate and prepare for the sacraments of initiation, normally at the Easter Vigil.

Children in the catechumenate make a preparation that is appropriate to their age level. They are expected to experience the conversion that a child their age could experience (RCIA, 253).

The shape of the catechumenate for children resembles that of adults. For example, they may celebrate the Rites of Acceptance and Election and a scrutiny. Most importantly, they celebrate all three sacraments at their initiation: Baptism, Confirmation, and Eucharist. Their condition as catechumens should not be confused with baptized children, "nor should they receive the sacraments of initiation in any sequence other than that determined in the ritual of Christian initiation" (NS, 19).

18. What is catechetical age?

Catechetical age means "the age at which one can be catechized." It is the expression used by the *Rite of Christian Initiation of Adults* to determine which children enter a *children's catechumenate*.

The Catholic Church offers two different rites of Baptism. The *Rite of Baptism for Children* is offered to infants and very young children. However, once a child is old enough to be catechized, he or she follows the *Rite of Christian Initiation of Adults*.

Although it seems odd to say such children are preparing for the rite of Baptism "for adults," our Church uses the rite of adult Baptism for children who have reached catechetical age. The *Code of Canon Law* treats such children as adults as far as Baptism is concerned (canon 852 §1).

No specific age is assigned. The judgment is left to parents, catechists, and pastors. We use other expressions to help determine this age. Children may be prepared for Reconciliation when they reach the "age of discretion"; that is, the age when they begin to know right from wrong. Children may be prepared for the first sharing of Communion when they reach the "age of reason"; that is, the age when they understand the difference between ordinary food and eucharistic food. And they may enter a catechumenate if they have reached "catechetical age," or the age at which they may be formed by catechesis. If pressed, we say that is about age seven. But it will be older or younger for individual children. A simple guideline is this: If an unbaptized child is old enough to be prepared for first Communion, he or she should enter the catechumenate for formation.

19. What if the parents, the catechists, or the pastor prefer that children of catechetical age defer their Confirmation until the children reach the diocesan age for confirming those young people baptized Catholic as infants?

Well, they are in violation of canon law. Canon 883 gives the priest the faculty of administering Confirmation when he baptizes a person who is no longer an infant, and canon 885 requires him to use that faculty. The reason? Because it is a favor granted the child. The Catholic Church permits Confirmation at the same age as first Confession, even younger in danger of death. Some people think that the age of Confirmation should be determined by the necessary catechesis, but the Church believes that the catechesis should be determined by the age of Confirmation.

20. Can a child be accepted into the catechumenate if the parents are not interested?

This is not a good idea. We really need the support of parents if a child's spiritual growth is to happen. The catechumenate is for children who seek Christian initiation "either at the direction of their parents or guardians or, with parental permission, on their own initiative" (RCIA, 252).

Parents have an important role to play in the formation of children. Their example is essential for the children's growth. Their participation in the catechesis of their children will make the children's catechumenate a rich experience.

If parents object to initiation, a parish should not proceed with the catechumenate for a young child. If parents grant permission but will not pledge their own participation, the community may seek assurance that someone (another relative, the godparent) will assist in the growth of the child. If parents give their full assent, they help the catechumenate achieve its goal.

In the case of infants, the Church permits their Baptism if there is a founded hope that the child will be brought up in the faith (canon 868). The law does not specify who brings the child up, but it does insist on hope. The same could apply to other young children as well.

21. What is the precatechumenate or period of evangelization?

The precatechumenate is the time of evangelization and properly pertains to the unbaptized. "Faithfully and constantly the living God is proclaimed and Jesus Christ whom he has sent for the salvation of all" (RCIA, 36). During this period the unbaptized first hear the Gospel, which challenges and consoles them. During this period candidates will become aware of God's activity in their lives.

Two principal dynamics are at work during this period: the questions brought by the candidates and the spiritual stories they tell.

Candidates will almost always have some questions about the Catholic Church: Why we do things our way. What we believe about moral behavior. What we believe about the pope, Mary, Reconciliation, the Mass, and so on. During this period, candidates deserve to have their questions answered according to their level of understanding. At the same time, it is important for the catechist to note what the questions are and why they seem important. The catechist can usually learn a great deal about the spiritual life of the candidate by asking about the questions they bring. The goal of this period is not to cover the basics about the Catholic Church. The goal is more rudimentary than that. It is to proclaim the Gospel (RCIA, 36–38).

Spiritual stories also tell a great deal about the candidates. During this period we invite them to reflect on why they have come to seek

Christ, where they might have found God before, and whether they see with new insight God's plan for their lives. The catechist will help bring out these stories for spiritual conversation. When we connect these stories to the Scriptures, we help the candidates find their place in salvation history (RCIA, 38).

Since the period of precatechumenate, properly speaking, pertains to the unbaptized, there is no "precatechumenate" for those who are already beyond the catechumenate by means of their Baptism. However, baptized candidates may also have questions to ask and spiritual stories to tell. They often find this period helpful to their spiritual growth. A mixed group of unbaptized and baptized candidates may have much to share with one another, but their different standings should not be confused (NS, 25, 30–31). Candidates may also be invited into a parish faith-sharing group where their stories can be shared.

Baptized candidates with a fuller background of catechesis and church life may not need this preliminary period. Take the example of a baptized candidate who for several years has attended weekly Mass with a Catholic spouse, participated in service opportunities, and fostered religious education with their children. Such a candidate may not need a preliminary period of inquiry at all.

This period carries an introductory tone. It need not cover a comprehensive survey of Christian teaching. That will follow in the next stage. It should provide initial spiritual discussion, introduction to members of the community, and the formation of a basic, foundational decision to follow Christ. There should not be a formal ritual at the beginning of this period. It just starts when the Spirit prompts the heart of a potential candidate (RCIA 39; NS, 1). For many, this period may be quite brief. If they come with some spiritual life, they may already have achieved the goals of the precatechumenate.

22. What happens at a precatechumenate session?

A precatechumenate session can take on different forms. Many parishes find success in the following suggestions:

The group meets either in the home of a parishioner or on church property. A home emphasizes the welcome we offer those who seek a deeper union with Christ and the communal dimension of the church. Some groups always meet in the same home; others meet in several homes over a period of time. In other situations, the parish complex offers the best space. The group has regular meetings, usually gathering weekly at an announced day and time.

Ideally, a precatechumenate meets throughout the entire year. Participants may join at any time and leave when they are ready. They need have no fixed program at this stage; they need not form a "class" that enters and leaves at a common time. In this way, whenever the parish becomes aware of someone who wishes a closer union with the church, he or she can attend a precatechumenate session within a week or a very short time. There is no time limit to the precatechumenate. It may be completed very briefly for those who are sure of their desire to enter the catechumenate. Or it may extend over a period of years while the candidate discerns whether or not this is the path toward which they are called.

Many parishes offer the precatechumenate only in the months before Christmas. The *Rite of Christian Initiation of Adults* never foresees this as a specific possibility nor as a dominant option. Offering precatechumenate during the same months each year simplifies matters for the parish trying to control staff and volunteer hours and to move a catechumenate group through stages together. But by offering this stage only once a year the parish neglects the ministry of spiritual guidance at other seasons. If potential catechumens are told, "Sessions begin in September," they may well wonder why the Holy Spirit stirred their hearts in February. The *Rite of Christian Initiation of Adults* suggests no beginning time of the precatechumenate. The book assumes that the precatechumenate is always active and present in a parish.

A typical session could include the following components:

- **A time of welcome.** We introduce ourselves and say something about why we are there.

- **A time of prayer.** We use one of the many forms of Christian prayer.

- **A time of questioning.** The questions brought by the candidates are given time. If the catechist does not know an answer, a more complete response may follow at the next session.

- **A time of storytelling.** The spiritual lives of candidates come to light as they share experiences from their recent and more remote past. Catechists help connect their stories to the Gospel.

- **A time of evangelization.** The catechist shares Christian belief in the existence of God, the life of Christ, and the activity of God in the world today.

- **A time of refreshment.** Snacks and drinks help create a community.

Alternative models for a session break from this routine. The group could perform some service activity together. A Catholic family may invite them over to share a meal and talk about what makes their home Christian. All could make a pilgrimage to some sacred place.

23. Can marital status keep someone from becoming Catholic?

In some cases marital status is an obstacle to sharing Communion in the Catholic Church. When Catholics enter a second marriage while the church presumes that the first is still binding, we ask them to abstain from Communion. A catechumen or candidate in this situation is ineligible for Communion and other sacraments in the Catholic Church.

Our church places a high value on Christian Marriage. Marriage symbolizes the permanent love that God has for us. Consequently, when two people marry for the first time—even if they are not Catholics—we assume they meant to enter into a permanent relationship. The Church's hesitancy to accept a second marriage comes from the value we place on every Marriage.

To become eligible for Communion, catechumens or candidates who have married more than once follow the same procedures as Catholics. They must obtain an annulment on prior marriages and convalidate their present marriage in the Catholic Church.

A convalidation resembles a wedding; however, most couples in this situation keep the ceremony fairly informal, inviting only a few family and friends. A priest or deacon presides over the ceremony—usually a wedding without Mass as found in the *Order of Celebrating Matrimony*. It takes place at church as soon as the two parties are free to marry.

Although these steps eliminate the obstacle to sharing Communion in the Church, they would be prudently accomplished before the Rite of Election. An inquirer still needing an annulment could be accepted as a catechumen. But it would be incorrect to baptize such a person or to receive into the Church a baptized candidate still needing an annulment, while withholding Communion. Without the convalidation, the non-Catholic party is eligible for neither Baptism, nor Confirmation, nor Communion.

Those who divorce are not automatically excluded from Communion. Entering a second marriage without an annulment of the first causes this discipline to happen. So if catechumens or candidates are divorced but not remarried, their marital status will not keep them from Communion in the Catholic Church. However, in prudence, they should learn what the Church will expect of them should they decide to marry.

24. What is an annulment?

An annulment is a declaration by the Church that a marriage previously thought to be spiritually binding is not. An annulment does not nullify a binding marriage. It asserts that the marriage in question never was binding, but this did not become evident until some time after the ceremony. An annulment does not affect the status of children.

To obtain an annulment one of the former partners makes a petition to a diocesan marriage tribunal. Every Catholic parish should assist with this service. The tribunal will invite testimony about the marriage. It obtains the necessary paperwork and investigates the nature of the relationship before, during, and after the marriage. A marriage may be declared null based on a number of factors, such as immaturity, deception, absence of commitment, or an invalid ceremony. Effective work on annulments requires the pastoral assistance of a compassionate minister.

Annulments can offer the opportunity for spiritual growth. Although the procedures may sound sterile, the process intends to help people review their past, face their troubles, and experience the grace of Christ at work within them. This very personal investigation actually offers an opportunity for catechumens and candidates to see how God has guided them through some difficult days in their past.

After a catechumen or candidate obtains an annulment, the partners convalidate their present marriage in the Catholic Church. To do so, they exchange their marital consent before a Catholic priest or deacon, just as any couple does at the wedding. Some parishes delay the convalidation until shortly before the Baptism or Reception. There is no need for delay. In fact, if one party is a Catholic, convalidation will enable that person to share Communion immediately, while the partner is still in formation.

PART 3:
CATECHUMENATE

25. How do we know when someone is ready to move from precatechumenate to the catechumenate?

Unbaptized persons who have attended precatechumenate sessions may enter the catechumenate when "the beginnings of the spiritual life and the fundamentals of Christian teaching have taken root" in them (RCIA, 42).

Notice that we do not ask much. They need not have a developed spiritual life and a thorough acquaintance with Christian teaching. They just need the beginnings and fundamentals. If they show some faith, if they express a desire to change their lives to follow Christ, if they begin to pray, to have a sense of Church and some experience with your local community, they are ready. The team should judge the outward indications of the catechumens' dispositions (RCIA, 43).

Candidates, of course, have already been baptized. Consequently, they do not have a precatechumenate and catechumenate properly called. Nonetheless, since many of them are experiencing a spiritual journey along with catechumens, they may enter a new stage of their formation whenever they have the desire to do so. We look for them to express their intention for Communion and to demonstrate aspects of their Christian life in their belief and activity. When they have done so, they are ready for the next stage.

26. What is a sponsor supposed to do?

Sponsors accompany unbaptized candidates seeking admission as catechumens (RCIA, 10). They should know the candidates well enough to stand for their character, faith, and intention. Throughout the period of the catechumenate they help introduce the catechumens to the Christian way of life.

Those who are already baptized should also have the assistance of a sponsor as they prepare for the Rite of Reception.

The eligibility for serving as a sponsor is spelled out in canon 874. For example, a person should be at least sixteen years old, though exceptions can be made. Only a Catholic who has been baptized, confirmed, and who has received Communion may serve as a sponsor. An unconfirmed Catholic does not qualify. The potential sponsor must also be leading a life of faith. Neither the father nor the mother may be the sponsor for their own child. Although many people believe that a Catholic in an invalid marriage is ineligible to serve as a sponsor, canon 874 does not automatically exclude them. However, they must be living a life of faith.

Canon 874 does not exclude a spouse from serving as a sponsor; however, the spouse already has a role: being the spouse. A different person usually will perform the functions of the sponsor more faithfully. The sponsor is not just someone who has inspired faith, but someone who will represent the entire Christian community, who discerns readiness, and who guides the new Catholic's faith in the future.

Your parish may establish additional guidelines for sponsors. Ideally, sponsors for your catechumens and candidates come from your parish, but sometimes members of other communities may serve, especially if they already have an influential relationship with those they sponsor. Sponsors should model the Christian life and introduce catechumens and candidates to the local community. They may also take part in discernment to determine who is ready to advance through the stages of the catechumenate. You may offer some kind of training for sponsors to clarify their role.

You may determine how frequently they should attend sessions. In many communities, sponsors attend the catechetical sessions throughout the period of formation. Their presence is essential at the liturgical rites where they play a role. Their real service takes place apart from formal sessions, when they spend time getting to know those whom they are sponsoring.

You have some freedom in establishing expectations of sponsors. Make sure you and the sponsors have a common understanding.

27. What is the difference between a sponsor and a godparent?

A godparent is the sponsor who accompanies an unbaptized person from the Rite of Election through initiation and during the period of mystagogy (RCIA, 11). The godparent may be different from the sponsor, but in many cases, the sponsor who begins to accompany a catechumen will finish as the godparent. Godparents begin their service at the Rite of Election—or the parish's Rite of Sending the Catechumens for Election.

The *Code of Canon Law* specifies who qualifies as a sponsor (canon 874). However, the English translation of the code does not distinguish between sponsors and godparents. Canon 874 more properly applies to godparents. There are no clear canonical guidelines for the person that RCIA 11 describes as a sponsor. Logically, the ideal person would meet the same requirements. Yet because the role comes to an end before the Rite of Election, an RCIA sponsor could perhaps be someone who does not meet all the standards of the RCIA godparent.

The godparents' testimony at the time of election is essential to discerning the catechumen's progress. Their presence at Baptism is vital to the exercise of their ministry.

Baptized candidates preparing for Reception have sponsors, not godparents. Godparents assist those needing Baptism, and candidates may already have had them. Some baptized candidates come from denominations that do not have godparents. But all candidates receive the service of sponsors at the Rite of Reception into the Full Communion of the Catholic Church.

28. What is the Rite of Acceptance into the Order of Catechumens?

The Rite of Acceptance into the Order of Catechumens formally establishes a relationship between the inquiring candidate and the Church. Those who are not baptized are accepted into the order of catechumens. As catechumens, they help constitute the Church. If they are engaged, they may marry in the Catholic Church (RCIA, 47). If they die they are entitled to a Catholic funeral (canon 1183). They will receive the prayers and support of the Church. In the Rite of Acceptance, catechumens state publicly their intention and the Church announces their first reception.

The ceremony has several parts (RCIA, 48–68). Outside or at the door of the church the presider greets the assembly and explains the ceremony. He asks the candidates to give their names and to explain what they are asking of God's Church. He then offers a brief catechesis, and the catechumens formally accept the Gospel for the first time. The presider then solicits the support of the sponsors and the assembly. The candidates are then signed with the cross, first on the forehead and then, optionally, on other parts of the body. This is one of the most memorable parts of the Rite of Acceptance. The presider prays for them, and from this point on, the rubrics refer to them as "catechumens." The presider invites them into the church to hear the Word of God. Before the readings begin, the presider explains the dignity of God's Word. After the homily, the new catechumens may receive a Bible or a pocket-sized booklet containing the four Gospels. The community prays for them and they are dismissed to reflect on the word and ritual. If this has taken place at a Mass, the assembly of the faithful remains in place to complete the Liturgy of the Eucharist.

Some adaptations to this and other rites may occur (General Introduction, 34–35; RCIA, 35).

29. What is the Rite of Welcoming?

The Rite of Welcoming the Candidates is an adaptation of the Rite of Acceptance, suitable for baptized candidates preparing for the Rite of Reception, Confirmation (when appropriate), and the first sharing of Communion (RCIA, 411). It was designed for Catholics with a valid Baptism but no further catechesis, and it is permitted for those with "relatively little Christian upbringing" (NS, 31). It was not designed for baptized candidates "who have lived as Christians" (NS, 31).

Welcoming the candidates is an optional rite created for use in the United States. The Rite of Acceptance into the Order of Catechumens, on the other hand, is part of the liturgy of the universal church and "is of the utmost importance" (RCIA, 41).

The ritual of welcoming is similar to that of Acceptance. Candidates are greeted inside the church at their places among the assembly. They give their names and explain what they are asking of the Church. They state their intent to prepare for Confirmation and Communion. Sponsors and the assembly voice their support. The candidates are signed with the cross as a reminder of their Baptism and receive the prayer of the community.

When the group preparing for these sacraments in your parish is a mixture of baptized and unbaptized candidates, you may follow a combined Rite of Acceptance and Welcoming (RCIA, 505–529). It is an adaptation of the adaptation created for use in the United States. It is also optional.

30. When should the Rites of Acceptance and Welcoming take place?

The ceremonies may take place during a Sunday celebration of the Eucharist so that members of the faithful are present. It may be celebrated at any time, and it may be offered several times a year, whenever candidates for Baptism and the Rite of Reception are ready to begin this stage of their spiritual journey (RCIA, 18.3, 44, 45, 414).

For children of catechetical age, the Rite of Acceptance may occur with a small gathering of family and friends apart from the Eucharist (RCIA, 260–261). However, if the children are not intimidated by the Sunday assembly, there is no reason to avoid a regularly scheduled weekend Mass.

31. Why does the Rite of Acceptance start at the door of the church?

The Rite of Acceptance begins at the door of the church in keeping with a custom dating back to the Middle Ages. Those who entered the catechumenate began this ritual outside the church, to signify their passage from outside to inside the community of believers. The rite may be celebrated elsewhere (RCIA, 48)—at a school or in some neutral area, for example. But the parish church usually makes the best location.

The symbol of crossing a threshold can be found in the story of the Baptism of Cornelius from Acts of the Apostles. Peter's first conversation with Cornelius happens outside the house. They cross the threshold to begin the discernment of faith and catechesis (10:27).

A group of the faithful gathers with the candidates and sponsors outside the church (RCIA, 48). When celebrating this rite in your parish, you may invite people to gather there before the liturgy begins. Or, once the faithful have assembled, you may invite them to go as a body to greet the unbaptized outside the church. Certain logistics need attention: adequate space for all to assemble, visibility of the ceremony, sound reinforcement so that the dialogue can be heard, and musicians to lead singing during the processions, for example. Having the faithful present for this part of the rite will permit them to demonstrate by their procession their interest and prayer for those who are seeking Baptism.

The Rite of Welcoming does not begin at the door of the church because the people we are welcoming have already been baptized. Instead, the candidates sit "in a prominent place among the faithful" (RCIA, 416). The difference in the beginning of the Rites of Acceptance and Welcoming is subtle. But it demonstrates our affirmation of the Baptism we share in common with other Christian churches.

In the adaptation for children, as with adults, the rite may take place at any suitable place. If that place is the church, the liturgy may begin outside the door (RCIA, 262, 269).

The symbolism of the door is enriched further by this distinction. Those who are unbaptized are making a passage into a direct relationship with the assembly of the faithful. Those who are baptized already share that relationship and need not make a passage or cross a threshold to establish it.

32. How should the candidates answer the question, "What do you ask of God's Church?"

The candidates are free to answer this question in their own words (RCIA, 50, 418, 509). A second question, based on those words, follows.

For the unbaptized the ritual proposes a simple response to the question, "What do you ask of God's Church?" "Faith." For the baptized the ritual suggests a descriptive response: "To be accepted as a candidate for catechetical instruction leading to Confirmation and Eucharist."

The questions may be rephrased. For example, the presider may ask, "What do you desire?" or "For what reason have you come?" or another leading question that will prompt a heartfelt reply.

The presider then asks a further question such as, "What does faith offer you?" The unbaptized candidate replies something like, "Eternal life."

The Rite of Welcoming does not suggest a second question for the baptized candidate (RCIA, 418), but one does appear in the combined Rites of Acceptance and Welcoming (RCIA, 509). The presider asks, "What does this period of formation offer you?" to which the candidate may respond, "A fuller sharing in the life of the Church."

In the Rite of Acceptance for children of catechetical age, an alternate series of questions is proposed (RCIA, 264). They intend to engage the children at their level of comprehension and moral development. These questions, beginning with "What do you want to become?" are influenced by earlier versions of the adult rite of becoming a catechumen. The same questions may be appropriate as adaptations in the adult rite as well.

Many communities invite the candidates to compose elaborated responses. To help them prepare for this, candidates may spend some time at a precatechumenate session or on a special day of retreat. You may ask them this question: "What do you ask of the Church as you make this step?" Give them time to journal about their response, to talk it over with their sponsor, or to discuss it with members of your team. If they will hear two questions in the liturgy, have them prepare their answers accordingly in two parts.

During the liturgy the candidates need not read an entire essay, but they may say a couple of sentences to explain to the assembly what they are asking. If they've given these questions some thought, their answers will be filled with meaning. The faithful need to hear what the candidates expect of them. The time spent in formulating this response before the liturgy will lend much significance to the celebration.

33. What is the first acceptance of the Gospel?

The first acceptance of the Gospel is the unbaptized candidates' first public declaration of their intention to follow Christ. Baptized candidates, because they have already accepted the Gospel, make a declaration of intent instead (RCIA, 419).

The presider who asks for this statement should phrase the question in accordance with the response the candidate gave to the question, "What do you ask of God's Church?" Building on that response, the presider may proclaim some aspect of the mystery of Christ, cite a passage from Scripture, clarify a point of catechesis, and then invite the candidate to state his or her readiness to accept the Gospel and its implications. Examples of this statement by the presider can be found in the ritual text (RCIA, 52, 511).

The presider should make the purpose of this statement clear. It should proclaim the mystery of Christ. It should relate that mystery to the candidate's desires. It should invite the affirmation from the candidate.

In the adaptation for children, the presider may offer a brief catechesis and invite the children to repeat the words of Christ as a sign of their assent: "Love God with all your heart and love one another as I have loved you" (RCIA, 264).

Some communities have introduced ritual adaptations for this part of the rite. For example, the crossbearer stands before the candidates. The presider takes the hands of the candidate in his own and places them on the cross with his, while he addresses each one and receives assent. The gesture can unite the acceptance of the Gospel with the acceptance of the cross.

Before moving on the presider secures the prayerful and exemplary support of the sponsors, parents (in the case of children), and the entire community (RCIA, 53, 265, 420, 513).

34. Why are the candidates signed with a cross?

During the Rite of Acceptance and the Rite of Welcoming, after the candidates express their desire to follow the Gospel, they are signed with the cross (RCIA, 54, 266, 421, 514). In the case of unbaptized candidates, they receive the cross for the first time as a sign that they are now marked by Christ, "branded" as a sheep in the divine flock. In the case of baptized candidates, they receive the cross as a reminder of their Baptism.

Christians have signed themselves with the cross since the early Church. It became a means of identification and sanctification. It reminds us of who we are and consecrates us for our ministry and life. The signing of those becoming catechumens has been part of our history also since the early Church.

There are several options for making the signation during the Rites of Acceptance and Welcoming. The presider traces the forehead, and then he or the sponsors trace the other crosses. The forehead alone may be signed, or several other senses as well. After each signation the assembly may sing an acclamation. The involvement of sponsors and assembly in this ritual demonstrates their participation in the formation of catechumens and candidates. Some communities move the liturgy indoors just before the signations so the assembly may more easily see and hear them, but the ritual envisions it outside if it involves unbaptized inquirers.

To make a pastoral distinction between the two groups in the combined rite, the number of crosses traced on the candidates may be fewer in number than those traced on the unbaptized.

After the signations, the Rite of Acceptance refers to the unbaptized candidates as "catechumens" for the first time. This ritual accepts them into the order, or community, of catechumens within the church.

35. Why does the invitation to the Celebration of the Word of God appear in the Rite of Acceptance but not in the Rite of Welcoming?

After the signations during the Rite of Acceptance, the presider invites the catechumens into the church building to hear the Word of God (RCIA, 60, 269). The invitation is omitted in the Rite of Welcoming.

By means of the signations in the Rite of Acceptance, the new catechumens have just entered a formal relationship with the faithful. The presider invites them to enter the church for the first time as catechumens. Their first experience there is hearing the Word of God.

The invitation to the Word symbolizes the formal beginning of Scripture-rooted catechesis. The Word of God will provide the foundation for catechesis as catechumens hear it proclaimed in the Sunday Scriptures. Prior to the Second Vatican Council, we used to call the first part of the Eucharist "the Mass of the catechumens." In the early Church, catechumens joined the faithful around the Scriptures, and all—the baptized and those in preparation for Baptism—feasted together at the table of God's Word.

During the Middle Ages catechumens received a formal presentation of the four Gospels as part of their preparation for Baptism. Deacons carrying the Gospels amid incense and candles processed into the church. They proclaimed the first words of each Gospel and the presider briefly explained the contents of the books. Today's catechumenate no longer includes this ritual. A vestige of it appears here in the simple invitation to catechumens to hear the Word of God.

In the case of baptized candidates, the Rite of Welcoming does not formally invite them to hear the Word. We assume that those who are baptized have already pledged themselves to Christ and have been hearing the Word and forming themselves by it. Besides, welcoming begins inside the church and needs no procession at this point. Consequently, the presider omits the formal invitation to the Word but explains instead the dignity of the word as it is proclaimed in the assembly of God's people (RCIA, 425). This explanation also occurs in the Rite of Acceptance once the catechumens have taken their place in the assembly of the faithful (RCIA, 61).

When celebrating the combined Rites of Acceptance and Welcoming, the liturgy begins outdoors and both groups hear the invitation to the Word of God (RCIA, 521). This simplifies the liturgy, but it blurs the distinction between catechumens and candidates. If your community has both unbaptized and baptized inquirers at the same time, there are other options to consider. You may celebrate with the two groups at two separate Masses the same weekend or on two completely different occasions. You may also omit altogether the Rite of Welcoming the baptized because it is optional.

36. Why may catechumens receive a book containing the Gospels or a cross?

Before the readings at the Rite of Acceptance, the catechumens may be given a cross (RCIA, 59). After the homily, they may be given a bible or a book containing the Gospels (RCIA, 64). These gifts signify their acceptance of the Gospel and the cross of Christ. The ceremonies are optional.

Baptized candidates may receive a Bible or Book of Gospels in the Rite of Welcoming (RCIA, 428). The liturgy does not suggest the gift of a cross. The meaning of this nuance is not clear. The optional presentation of a physical cross to catechumens would strengthen the symbol of their signations (RCIA, 74). The omission of this presentation for candidates probably implies that the baptized have already accepted it. Yet they may receive the gesture of a cross in the signations during the Rite of Welcoming. Furthermore, if the liturgy assumes the baptized have familiarity with the cross, it could also assume their familiarity with the Gospels. Yet a Book of the Gospels may be presented to candidates as a ritual gift.

The adaptation for children suggests only a book containing the Gospels (RCIA, 273). It never mentions giving a cross. In some cases, though, it may be appropriate and appreciated.

When the rites are combined, any of the gifts may be given (RCIA, 525). Again, this fuses catechumens and candidates, but in this case, the distinction may be harder to defend because both groups may receive signations. If the parish wishes to make a distinction, it may consider presenting Gospels to all and crosses to catechumens.

In the presentation of the book, the presider may say something appropriate such as, "Receive the Gospel of Jesus Christ, the Son of God." The catechumens and candidates may respond in whatever way they wish.

Several options exist here. Some communities have the director of the catechumenate or a catechist make the presentation (RCIA, 16). Some parishes give a physical book, one which may be used throughout formation. This may be done in silence. Or the one presenting may choose words to fit the responses from the opening dialogue, "What do you ask of God's Church?" For example, "Receive the word of God, which will guide your quest for faith." Catechumens and candidates may respond with a gesture or with words such as "Thanks be to God." Other parishes present the lectionary to the catechumens and candidates for them to kiss, touch, or reverence by lowering their head. Some present a cross (to be carried, worn around the neck, or pinned to the lapel) with a similar proclamation; for example, "Receive the cross of our Lord Jesus Christ in whom you will find hope." Catechumens and candidates may respond with words or a gesture, or they may make no response.

Again, all these gifts are optional. The gift of the Gospels and cross are particularly significant for those who are truly accepting Christ for the first time in their lives. Those unfamiliar with the Bible, those who have never owned a Bible, and those who have never kept a cross in their homes will find in these gifts a significant entrance to Catholic piety and to the Christian way of life.

37. Why do we dismiss catechumens at Mass?

We dismiss catechumens at Mass because they do not yet participate in the Eucharist (RCIA, 75.3).

The early Church began the custom of dismissing catechumens from the Eucharist. At the time many religions of the world had secretive elements. Only members were permitted to participate in their worship. Christianity was no exception. Only the baptized could celebrate the Eucharist. Those in formation for Baptism attended the first part of the celebration, in which they could fully participate. Then they were dismissed and the faithful remained for the Eucharist.

The practice expressed the role of the faithful. The Eucharist depended on their participation. If the liturgy were to permit spectators, anyone could attend the celebration. But it was the faithful who professed the Creed, the faithful who offered prayers, the faithful who made sacrifice, the faithful who called God their Father, the faithful who exchanged the kiss of peace, the faithful who shared the Eucharist, and the faithful who were dismissed as a body to bear witness to Christ. They alone remained for the Eucharist, not as spectators but as participants in ministry.

Today attendance at Eucharist is more open. If visitors come for the celebration we generally admit them, no matter their faith. The Eucharist is no longer a secret; it is broadcast to billions on television and across the internet.

Consequently, many people feel the dismissal of catechumens looks rude. If others do not leave, they reason, surely catechumens should remain. However, the emphasis falls not on "dismissal from," but on "dismissal to." Catechumens are not so much dismissed from the liturgy as they are dismissed to a catechetical session. This gives their dismissal a better shaped purpose. Pastoral experience shows that catechumens welcome the added time to reflect on the Word and appreciate the support and prayer of the community as they leave.

The dismissals of the Roman liturgy are meant to bring order to the celebration and to define the calling of the participants. The dismissal of children from the Liturgy of the Word lets them hear the readings proclaimed and preached at a more engaging level.

The dismissal of the assembly at the end of the Mass sends the faithful out into the world. The dismissal of catechumens offers them an occasion to reflect on the Word and to prepare their hearts for full participation in the sacraments.

38. Should candidates be dismissed at Mass?

The rite never calls for the dismissal of baptized candidates at the Eucharist. However, in practice many parishes do dismiss them.

Their dismissal never appears in the ritual text because they are among the baptized, among the faithful who share in the prayer of the second half of the Mass. Baptized, they already believe the Creed, support the prayer "of the faithful," are counted among the sisters and brothers who pray "Our Father," and exchange the sign of Christian peace. However, since they are outside the full communion of the Catholic Church, they do not yet share in the Eucharist.

Many candidates prefer to be dismissed with the catechumens since they cannot share Communion with the Catholic faithful. However, by remaining with the community of the faithful, they exercise a purpose there: to join the prayer of the Body of Christ.

39. How does the dismissal happen?

The dismissal usually takes place after the homily of the Mass. The presider says something like, "Catechumens, go in peace, and may the Lord remain with you always" (RCIA, 67).

The ritual text assigns this direction to the presider. However, it appeared among the deacon's duties in the early history of the Church. In some parishes deacons dismiss catechumens, as they dismiss the faithful at the end of the service (see RCIA, 15).

Just before the dismissal, the catechumens may step forward, and the presider may offer a prayer of exorcism or blessing (RCIA, 94 or 96).

The dismissal should happen reverently and with respect. The presider or deacon may call the catechumens forward before addressing them. A catechist (who participates in another complete celebration of the Eucharist) may lead the catechumens from the church. The catechist may carry the Book of the Gospels as the deacon or reader does in the entrance procession. Some communities express their support for the departing catechumens by singing a refrain. The catechist who leads the catechumens from the church may take the group to a separate room where they begin their catechetical session for the day. At the conclusion of the Eucharist, sponsors may join the catechumens and the catechist.

40. What is catechesis?

Catechesis is the fulfillment of Jesus' command to teach all nations. It follows the initial proclamation and reception of the Word and builds upon faith to form the believer in the Gospel. The *General Directory for Catechesis* (Congregation of the Clergy, 1997) explains its purpose in full.

Catechesis may take many forms. It educates about the Gospel, but it also shapes hearts to conform them to Christ. It also takes place in the presence of Christian worship, community, and ministry, when those who have heard the Gospel place it in action.

During the period of the catechumenate, catechumens are formed in four ways.

- They receive a suitable catechesis, gradual and complete, accommodated to the liturgical year.
- They become familiar with the Christian way of life.
- They participate in suitable liturgical rites.
- They learn how to spread the Gospel with others (RCIA, 75).

This fourfold purpose of Christian formation also describes four pillars upon which the Christian life is built: catechesis, community, worship, and mission. All four pillars are catechetical in some way, although the first is defined more narrowly as "catechesis."

41. When should catechesis take place?

Catechesis for catechumens should take place regularly throughout their period of formation. Two alternate models commonly appear in parishes.

In one, the catechumens are dismissed from the Eucharist into a catechetical session. They spend a good part of their Sunday in formation based on the Word of God just proclaimed to the full assembly. They begin with spiritual reflection on the Scriptures and the homily. Then they receive additional catechesis about the Church, as inspired by those Scriptures.

In the other model, catechumens dismissed from the Eucharist reflect on the Scriptures for a while and then go home. They return later in the week (a weeknight, perhaps) for a separate catechetical session.

In either case, sponsors generally attend the second part, so they may help the catechumens integrate the catechesis into their lives.

The expression "lectionary catechesis" or "lectionary-based catechesis" refers to a method of rooting the catechesis in the Scriptures of the day. It responds to the request that catechesis be "accommodated to the liturgical year" (RCIA, 16, 75.1). It fulfills the desire of Pope Paul VI that all the faithful regard Sacred Scripture "as an abiding fountain of spiritual life, as the principal basis for the handing on of Christian doctrine, and finally as the core of all theological formation" (Apostolic Constitution *Roman Missal*, 1969). Lectionary catechesis treats themes such as forgiveness, salvation, and ethics as the Scriptures of the day and the liturgical year invite. Instead of starting on page one of a catechetical text, the catechist starts with the Scriptures. As the liturgical year "unfolds the whole mystery of Christ" (*Constitution on the Sacred Liturgy*, 102), so does catechesis.

In preparing a session, the catechist will examine the lectionary, the needs of the catechumens, and the needs of the Church. The lectionary may propose several themes. The selection of one or more may rely on the other factors. These particular catechumens may need more time with forgiveness, while last year's catechumens needed more time with the Eucharist, for example. Also, the Church asks that the catechesis be "gradual and complete" (RCIA, 75.1). So if the group has not yet explored some important dimensions of the faith, the needs of the Church may prompt another theme for their development.

42. Who leads the catechesis?

The catechesis may be led by a priest, deacon, or catechist (RCIA, 16, 76). In practice, a catechist usually leaves the church with the catechumens during the dismissal in order to lead the session.

Catechists receive formation by whatever means the diocese or parish may offer. You do not have to know it all to be a catechist. But you should be willing to find out what you don't know. After some years of service, you will be surprised how much you are able to share with those who seek a deeper relationship with Jesus Christ.

43. How does a sample catechetical session look?

A sample catechetical session probably has three main components: a reflection on the Word, catechetical formation, and an experience of prayer. It may also include some service and community building.

The group may gather immediately following the dismissal, but in some communities, this is impractical. For example, in a parish with only one weekend Eucharist, the catechist may not be free to attend another celebration. If the catechist will remain with the assembly of the faithful throughout the Eucharist at which the catechumens are dismissed, the catechumens may begin this process on their own. Or they may meet with the catechist after the Eucharist or even on another day.

The catechist will then lead a reflection on the Word. Someone may proclaim one or more of the Scriptures again. The group may sing the refrain from the responsorial psalm. Then a discussion may take place about what the catechumens heard in the Scripture and the homily. Questions may be raised. Insights may be shared. Above all, this part of the session lets the Word of God permeate the catechumens and deepen their faith.

Sponsors may join the group for the second part. The catechist will lead a session that expands the catechumens' understanding. This is the period in which a "gradual and complete" catechesis (RCIA, 75.1) should take place.

Prayer may be included in the session. It may come at any time and take any form. During this period the Church's rites will purify and strengthen the catechumens (RCIA, 75.3).

At times the group may decide to perform some act of service together out of Christian charity. They may also share refreshments and enjoy one another's company, keeping the spirit of Christian gladness and support (RCIA, 75.2 and 4).

Here is an example of what a Sunday morning might look like:

9:00   Liturgy of the Word with the faithful gathered for Eucharist

9:30   Dismissal of catechumens, reflection on the Word

10:00   Catechetical session with sponsors, time for prayer

11:00   Adjourn

44. What are the minor rites?

The minor rites are prayer services suitable for the period of the catechumenate (RCIA, 79). They usually take place in a Celebration of the Word. They may include prayers of exorcism, blessings, and the anointing of catechumens. These rites are called "minor" because they are not designed for the Sunday Eucharist, but are celebrated on other occasions, for example after a catechetical session or on a weekday.

The Presentations of the Creed and the Lord's Prayer and the Ephphetha Rite, ceremonies that occur during the Period of Purification and Enlightenment, may also be anticipated and moved to this period. The framers of the catechumenate received concerns that this stage of formation had too few rituals and the next stage (purification and enlightenment) had too many. For this reason it is permitted to celebrate the presentations earlier. Their full significance, however, will be more clearly seen when they occur in proximity to Baptism.

45. What are Celebrations of the Word?

Celebrations of the Word are prayer experiences for catechumens based on readings from Scripture (RCIA, 81). They may keep the spirit of the liturgical season and contribute to the catechumens' experience of Christian worship. Some catechumens may need more experience with the Word even before attending the first part of Mass; some forms of the word celebrations are meant to assist them (RCIA, 82–83). If catechumens are not gathering with the assembly on Sunday for the Liturgy of the Word, they should gather themselves on Sunday so that they may begin to grasp the importance of this Christian day.

In one form, these celebrations are events especially for catechumens. In this case, the Word celebration occurs apart from the Sunday Eucharist, and some members of the faithful may join in prayer.

In another form, the Word celebration is the Liturgy of the Word within the Eucharist. In this case, the catechumens who participate in the first part of Sunday Mass are actually engaging in a Celebration of the Word as envisioned by the period of the catechumenate.

In a third form, a Celebration of the Word may be appended to a catechetical instruction. In this way the catechetical session is reinforced with a formal time of prayer (RCIA, 84). The Celebration of the Word may take place in this way: A song may open the prayer. Readings, psalms, and a homily may follow. Some other rite may then conclude the gathering—a blessing, for example (RCIA, 85–89).

46. What is an exorcism?

An exorcism is a petition for deliverance from the power of evil. Exorcisms appear in the Roman Catholic liturgy in three different forms.

The most infamous form of exorcisms concerns the rare cases in which personal demonic possession is suspected. These are called "major exorcisms." The rite of major exorcism calls upon the triumphant power of Jesus to overtake the possession by Satan. The ritual includes statements addressed to the devil, commanding the Evil One to flee. This kind of exorcism has received much attention in the media, but is used very little. Today many cases once thought to be demonic possession can be attributed to physical or psychological ailment, and other methods of healing can be employed.

There are two other forms of exorcism that are used more frequently in the Church: "minor exorcisms" and "exorcisms". Among the prayer services appropriate for catechumens are Liturgies of the Word that include a minor exorcism (RCIA, 90). They do not presume that the catechumen suffers personal demonic possession. They simply acknowledge the prebaptismal state. In that state, before the catechumens receive the sanctifying grace of Christ in Baptism, they are more susceptible to the attitudes, opinions, behaviors, and powers of evildoing. Minor exorcisms are prayers addressed to God, not imprecations leveled against the devil. They aim to free the catechumens from error, sin—whatever will keep them from accepting Christ.

Exorcisms take place during the scrutinies. They perform much the same function as minor exorcisms: They pray to God that those preparing for Baptism may be freed from the spirit of evil and filled with the Spirit of Christ.

An echo of the exorcisms occurs in the rite of infant Baptism. The exorcism that precedes the Baptism derives from the scrutiny.

47. Who can lead an exorcism?

Minor exorcisms may be led by a priest, deacon, or qualified catechist appointed by the bishop (RCIA, 12, 16, 91). Lay catechists, therefore, may lead a minor exorcism, but the liturgy envisions that the bishop will have deputed them to this task.

A minor exorcism may take place at the end of a catechetical session or even privately to individual catechumens in some special need (RCIA, 92). The priest may offer one to the catechumens at Mass just after the homily—whether or not they are dismissed from the assembly at that time. The one who leads the prayer extends his or her hands over the catechumens (RCIA, 94).

Exorcisms during the scrutinies, however, are to be led by a priest or a deacon only (RCIA, 145)

48. What are the blessings of the catechumens?

The blessings of the catechumens are prayers for courage, joy, and peace (RCIA, 95–97). The minister is a priest, deacon, or qualified catechist appointed by the bishop. Whereas the exorcisms pray for the removal of negative influences, blessings pray for the arrival of positive influences.

The blessings may be given within a word service. The presider extends hands over the group of catechumens and may impose hands on them individually as well. Hand laying and the tone of the prayers help distinguish them from exorcisms. Blessings may be given at the end of a catechetical session, within a word service, or at Mass after the homily.

49. When can we use the oil of catechumens?

The oil of catechumens may be used at any time during the period of the catechumenate. It may be administered during a service of the Word, as part of a catechetical session, or after the homily at Mass (RCIA, 98–103).

In keeping with the church's tradition, the presider for this anointing is a priest or a deacon. He anoints the catechumen on the breast, on both hands, or on other parts of the body. In the early Church, the minister anointed the entire body of naked catechumens. Today we observe decorum and anoint only part of the body.

The ritual symbolizes the catechumens' need for God's help and strength. It thus represents a situation similar to the exorcism. It demonstrates our desire to protect the catechumen from evil, as we sometimes use oil in daily life to protect against injury.

The oil of catechumens is blessed each year by the bishop at the Chrism Mass. However, if you run low, a priest may bless oil within this rite. The tradition calls for olive oil, but any plant oil may be blessed (canon 847.1).

Catechumens may be anointed more than once (100). Throughout the course of the catechumenate, if several anointings seem appropriate, the priest or deacon may administer them on one or more of the catechumens.

The *Roman Missal* (48) indicates two other occasions for anointing with the oil of catechumens: the preparation rites of Holy Saturday and just before the Baptisms at the Easter Vigil. However, in the United States, the conference of bishops has approved the omission of the oil of catechumens on those occasions (RCIA, 33.7).

50. Why does the Period of Purification and Enlightenment coincide with Lent?

The Period of Purification and Enlightenment usually coincides with Lent because during this time catechumens make their final preparation for Baptism at Easter (RCIA, 138–139). The name of this period explains its significance. Catechumens undergo a spiritual preparation, purifying their lives and enlightening their hearts.

However, the season of Lent has a double purpose. It not only prepares catechumens for Baptism. It also prepares the faithful for the renewal of their commitment to Christ. The Second Vatican Council desired to restore this double focus.

Many of the faithful know Lent as a time of penitence. It is the season for self-denial and renewal. Lent originated as a prebaptismal period of preparation for catechumens, during which the faithful were invited to join them in spiritual exercises of prayer and fasting. When participation in the catechumenate waned in the Middle Ages, the spiritual exercises for the faithful remained, leaving the Church a Lent with penance but normally without catechumens. Now the double purpose is back.

Purification and enlightenment coincide with Lent to restore baptismal preparation to its proper place.

PART 4:
PURIFICATION
AND
ENLIGHTENMENT

51. What is conversion?

Conversion is turning one's heart, mind, soul, and strength toward Christ. Catechumens experience conversion when they decide to let their faith in Christ lead their lives. It changes their attitudes, their understanding, their prayer, and their behaviors. The *Rite of Christian Initiation of Adults* assumes that prior to becoming catechumens, these individuals led lives apart from Christ. Their conversion places Christ at the center of their lives, with the Gospel as the guide for making their decisions.

This conversion will be scrutinized, purified, and enlightened throughout the season of Lent. Immediately before Baptism this conversion will be ritualized when the presider formally asks those to be baptized to renounce Satan. They are speaking aloud their decision to convert from their former way of life and to give all to follow Christ.

52. What is discernment?

Discernment is the process by which the community measures the conversion of catechumens. Before someone may be accepted for Baptism, the community must make a judgment about the individual's readiness (RCIA, 121). Conversion should be demonstrable. It should be evident from the lives of the catechumens that their desire for change has taken hold of them. Their behaviors, attitudes, and opinions may all be examined for the existence of a conversion of heart. Even before the Rite of Acceptance, the catechumenate team judges the outward indications of inward dispositions (RCIA, 43).

We not only have the right to judge catechumens, we have the responsibility. "The Church judges their state of readiness and decides on their advancement toward the sacraments of initiation" (RCIA, 119). In fact, all involved with the preparation of catechumens, including the assembly of the faithful, "should, after considering the matter carefully, arrive at a judgment about the catechumens' state of formation and progress" (RCIA, 121). As members of the faithful, we judge the readiness of those who wish to take their place among us.

Some people don't like the word "judge." Well, you judge people before dating them, before hiring them, before confiding in them, and before buying from them. Yes, Jesus said, "Judge not and you shall not be judged" (Mt 7:1; Lk 6:37; see Jn 8:7). But he also carefully selected his twelve apostles (e.g., Mt 10:1; Mk 3:14; and Lk 6:13). It would be irresponsible for us not to form basic judgments about the character of the people we meet.

Ultimately, the judgment is God's. We the Church exercise our judgment in faith that it has discerned the will of God.

53. How do you know when someone is ready for Baptism?

Catechumens are ready for Baptism when they are ready for the Rite of Election. They are ready for the Rite of Election if they "have undergone a conversion in mind and in action" and "developed a sufficient acquaintance with Christian teaching as well as a spirit of faith and charity" (RCIA, 120). They also must have the intention to celebrate initiation.

The Period of Purification and Enlightenment offers spiritual preparation to those called to Baptism. Consequently, the judgment about readiness for Baptism really belongs prior to the Rite of Election, not just prior to Baptism. The final weeks of preparation are not the time to cram in everything the catechumens have not yet learned. This is a time of retreat and recollection for those who have learned about Christ, who have undergone conversion, who can demonstrate that conversion in their actions and spirit, and who firmly desire Baptism.

You know they are ready if they have all that before the Rite of Election. All involved with preparing the catechumens make a deliberation prior to the Rite of Election. Catechumens may also take part. The deliberation may take various forms (RCIA, 122), but it should create the opportunity for those who know the catechumens to testify about their spiritual progress.

At a minimum, the pastor consults with those responsible for the formation of catechumens. They should discuss the spiritual growth of each catechumen, one by one. They should also solicit opinions from sponsors and godparents. Such conversations are best in person, but any means of communication is better than no communication. Discerning readiness means more than checking a record of attendance at catechetical sessions. It seeks information about the catechumen's faith, speech, and actions at church, at home, at work, and at play.

If the deliberation reveals that catechumens are not ready, they may be called to Baptism at a later time. If you think someone should receive Baptism at some other time of year apart from the Easter Vigil, you should obtain permission from your bishop before doing so (RCIA, 331).

Parishes should avoid automatically approving all catechumens for the Rite of Election without any discernment. This tendency especially threatens parishes with a fixed period for the catechumenate, for example, from early December through the First Sunday of Lent. The catechumenate has no fixed length. Those in formation remain in formation until they are ready. It may take more than a few months. The US bishops recommend it last at least one year (NS, 6). The period may even take several years (RCIA, 7.2). A conscientious parish will make year-round formation available for those who remain in the catechumenate for a length of time.

54. What issues could keep someone from Baptism?

Sometimes people are not ready to be baptized. One important indicator is their willingness to profess faith in the articles of the Creed. If they have problems with some of the core teaching of our faith—that God created the world, that Jesus is the Son of God, that there is life after death, for example—they are clearly not ready for Baptism. Other elements of our faith are just as important, but not included in the Creed: belief in the real presence of Christ in the Eucharist, for example, and belief that the Church is the Body of Christ. If catechumens cannot affirm these beliefs, they are not ready for Baptism, nor even for the Rite of Election.

Some may express hesitation over the Sacrament of Reconciliation. Here you discern whether the hesitation concerns belief in the forgiveness of sins or discomfort with the form of Reconciliation. If they deny that the Sacrament of Reconciliation fulfills the Church's mission of forgiveness, they face a more serious difficulty than embarrassment over confessing sins to a priest. Good pastoral care can often help a catechumen overcome discomfort.

Sometimes there are behavioral issues, especially concerning the Church's sexual morality. You may have a catechumen who cohabits with a partner or one who has entered a gay marriage. Although these behaviors are a step removed from the elements of faith professed in the Creed, they nonetheless create dissonance with the Catholic application of our beliefs. Once again, good pastoral care will lead such catechumens into a frank discussion about the disparity between their actions and the expectations of the Catholic community. If in the local confessor's judgment these behaviors would exclude such individuals from receiving the Eucharist, it would not be appropriate to baptize.

In other instances, catechumens may find that they do not regularly observe some Catholic pieties: for example, devotion to Mary and the saints, charismatic prayer, or adoration of the Blessed Sacrament. The possible pieties among Catholics are numerous, and you can help catechumens understand that some aspects of religious life, which may be very "Catholic" to the media, permit a freer range of observance. You do not have to pray the Rosary every day to be a good Catholic, although the custom is certainly praiseworthy. Of more concern would be reticence to participate in the Sunday Eucharist.

55. Under what circumstances does adult initiation happen apart from Lent and Easter?

In exceptional circumstances adult initiation of the unbaptized may take place apart from Lent and Easter in a full (RCIA, 26) or abbreviated rite (RCIA, 331–339). Permission comes from the local bishop (RCIA, 34.2 and 4), and the US bishops have requested a limited use of the abbreviated catechumenate (NS, 20–21).

Examples of extraordinary circumstances include sickness, old age, change of residence, long absence for travel (RCIA, 332), or even an impending annulment. If a candidate for initiation in your community faces such a condition, you may obtain permission from the bishop to celebrate initiation on another occasion. Contacting the bishop may seem odd, but the procedure stresses his role as the primary minister of Baptism for the diocese and the importance of celebrating adult Baptism at Easter.

The rite apart from Lent and Easter has several possible forms. If the person's condition permits it, "the structure of the entire rite, with its properly spaced intervals, remains the same" (RCIA, 26). The Rite of Acceptance is followed by a Rite of Election six weeks before a Sunday celebration of the rites of initiation (RCIA, 27–30). If this is not possible, the abbreviated form of the entire rite may be used (RCIA, 340–369). When time and circumstances permit, this form may be expanded where possible (RCIA, 334). It may also be further adapted for persons in danger of death (RCIA, 370–399).

56. What is the Rite of Sending?

The Rite of Sending is the parish celebration that sends catechumens to the cathedral for the Rite of Election (RCIA, 106–117). It is an optional rite created for use in the United States. If the Rite of Election takes place in the parish, there is no Rite of Sending. The Rite of Sending was developed to let members of the local community experience some aspect of the Rite of Election, because the ceremony at the cathedral can usually accommodate very few of the faithful from each parish.

If baptized candidates are attending a rite of call to continuing conversion at the cathedral, they may also participate in a Rite of Sending at the parish (RCIA, 434–445). Parishes with both catechumens and candidates may celebrate a combined Rite of Sending (RCIA, 530–546). These adaptations of the optional Rite of Sending the Catechumens for Election are also optional.

This simple rite takes place after the homily of a Sunday Mass immediately preceding the Rite of Election. The catechumens and candidates are presented to the presider. Their godparents, who take part in a ritual for the first time, and sponsors give testimony on their behalf. Some communities invite open testimony by others in the assembly. The presider offers a prayer over them and they may be dismissed in the usual way.

57. What is the Rite of Election?

The Rite of Election or Enrollment of Names is the recognition of God's choice to call the catechumens for immediate initiation into the Church (RCIA, 118–119). It usually coincides with the First Sunday of Lent, closes the period of the catechumenate, and begins the proximate preparation for Baptism at Easter. Catechumens who undergo this rite are called "elect" during the Period of Purification and Enlightenment. The Rite of Election for children is optional (RCIA, 277–280), but children may be invited to participate in the diocesan celebration.

Two elements are key to the celebration: the testimony of godparents and catechists, and the inscription of the names of the elect (RCIA, 129–137).

Testimony occurs in the form of affirmation by the godparents and the assembly. After the catechumens are presented, the presider (usually the bishop) asks godparents if they consider the candidates worthy for initiation. This question and answer presumes that some deliberation has taken place prior to this moment. The Rite of Election brings to a ritual moment the decision that these catechumens are ready for Baptism.

The inscription is made in the Book of the Elect. The names recorded there are the names by which the elect will be baptized.

The enrollment may take different forms. Ideally catechumens inscribe their names in the Book of the Elect at this point in the ceremony. Godparents or someone from the catechumenate team may write the names as the catechumens call them out. In some dioceses, catechumens write their names in their parishes at the Rite of Sending, and the names are presented at this point of the ritual. In that case it is still the presenting of the names—not the Rite of Sending—that constitutes their enrollment.

Godparents may also sign the book (RCIA, 123). This follows a practice from the early Church. It has the advantage of validating the importance of the godparents' testimony. It has the disadvantage of eclipsing the significance of the signature of the elect. It may also unfavorably lengthen the service. It is not appropriate for the bishop to sign the book.

After the enrollment, the presider announces that the catechumens are members of the elect. All offer prayers on their behalf, and if there is no Eucharist at this celebration, all are dismissed.

Baptized candidates do not celebrate the Rite of Election because election is a prebaptismal acknowledgment of the names God is calling to life in Christ. However, candidates may be invited to participate in the Rite of Calling the Candidates to Continuing Conversion, an optional ceremony modeled on the Rite of Election (RCIA, 446–458). The *Rite of Christian Initiation of Adults* also provides an adaptation that combines the integral Rite of Election with the optional rite of calling (RCIA, 547–561).

58. Why does the Rite of Election take place at the cathedral?

The Rite of Election takes place at the cathedral because of the bishop's role. The bishop is ultimately responsible for deciding who is among the elect (RCIA, 121), although in practice he relies on the testimony of others working more closely with catechumens.

Actually, the bishop is also the primary minister of Baptism itself (General Introduction, 12). In the early Church the bishop presided for all the Baptisms of the diocese. Today, given the size of dioceses, this has become impractical, and Baptisms take place more frequently in parishes where the local community can get to know the catechumens. A vestige of the original practice remains in the celebration of the Rite of Election at the cathedral. But in the early Church, all the ceremonies—not just election—would have taken place there.

If for some reason a catechumen who desires Baptism cannot be present for the Rite of Election at the cathedral on the First Sunday of Lent, you may consider offering the rite at the parish. This option is clearly permitted when all of initiation takes place at a different time of year (RCIA, 26, 126–127). Given the significance of this rite for the unbaptized, it would be prudent for parishes to provide this opportunity for those absent from the cathedral celebration.

If catechumens are unable to participate in the diocesan Rite of Election, the bishop may delegate a priest or a deacon to celebrate the liturgy in his stead (RCIA, 12, 121). For example, a pastor could send a letter to the bishop, requesting delegation to enroll one or more catechumens among the elect. If there is a diocesan Book of the Elect, he should borrow it for the occasion.

The Rite of Election should not be omitted for those who are following the normal course of initiation. There are exceptional circumstances when all of initiation is more compressed, but as a rule, all catechumens should participate in the Rite of Election.

59. What is the Book of the Elect?

The book of the elect is a book of empty pages upon which are inscribed the names of those chosen for the sacraments of initiation.

It may be a large book with pages scored or unscored, ready to receive signatures. It may be reused from year to year or replenished anew each year. It may be small enough for the parish or large enough for the entire diocese. It may be a diocesan binder into which are clasped the punched pages signed in parishes. Some publishers offer books of the elect for sale. Some dioceses have fashioned their own.

60. Who should sign the Book of the Elect?

Catechumens who will be initiated several weeks after the rite should sign the book. Catechumens who will remain in formation longer wait until they begin their own proximate preparation for Baptism, probably the following year. Through the Rite of Election these catechumens are now called the elect.

The liturgy does not invite baptized candidates preparing for the Rite of Reception to sign the book. They are already baptized, and the signing is a prebaptismal ritual indicating one's readiness for Baptism. It is inappropriate for candidates to sign the book.

Godparents may sign the book with the elect. It is optional.

61. Should the book be signed at the parish or at the cathedral?

Ideally the Book of the Elect is signed at the cathedral. But for pastoral reasons the book may be signed at the parish. For example, those preparing the diocesan liturgy may judge that having all catechumens sign the book during the Rite of Election would unduly prolong the ceremony.

However, because this is one of the key moments in the Rite of Election, it is preferable to allow time for the enrollment even though it may lengthen the proceedings. Others prefer to have the book signed at the parish so that more members of the local community may witness it. Nonetheless, the enrollment that takes place during the Rite of Election carries more significance.

62. May the Rite of Election be repeated?

In many dioceses the Rite of Election is repeated. Some cathedrals cannot hold the numbers attending in a single event. Cathedrals that are distant from many parts of the diocese make travel impractical. For these reasons the rite may be repeated on the same day or over a period of days. It may also take place in parishes. However, it should be celebrated at the cathedral on or close to the First Sunday in Lent for those to be baptized the following Easter (RCIA, 126).

Each catechumen, of course, celebrates election only once.

63. Is the Sacrament of Reconciliation necessary for catechumens and candidates?

Celebration of the Sacrament of Reconciliation is not necessary for catechumens. In fact, because they are unbaptized, they are not eligible for any other sacrament, including Reconciliation. Baptism is not only their first sacrament, it constitutes forgiveness of sins. Catechumens need not confess their sins to a priest prior to Baptism because Baptism forgives all their sins.

Stories have been told of priests who interrupted the Easter Vigil to hear the confession of the newly baptized before they share Communion. Such behavior, while wanting to honor the Church's tradition of Reconciliation before Communion, is completely inappropriate and reflects a poor understanding of the effects of Baptism.

Some catechumens may express the desire to confess their sins. The Sacrament of Reconciliation brings spiritual relief for those who celebrate it fully. Catechumens may tell their sins to a confessor if they would find that helpful, as long as everyone understands that this is different from sacramental Reconciliation. Since this does not constitute the sacrament, catechumens could acknowledge their guilt before any spiritual director—even a catechist or sponsor. However, in no way should the team make this an expectation.

After initiation the newly baptized may celebrate Reconciliation as the Spirit moves them. You could also help organize a celebration of Reconciliation sometime after initiation for those who wish to experience its comfort.

Candidates should celebrate Reconciliation prior to the Rite of Reception with Confirmation and Eucharist (RCIA, 482; NS, 27). This prepares them for sharing Communion with the Catholic faithful. They may take part in a communal penance service, or if they wish more time to discuss their sins they may prefer a private celebration.

64. What is the Penitential Rite for candidates?

The Penitential Rite for candidates is an optional ceremony modeled on the scrutinies to help candidates make their spiritual preparation for the Rite of Reception (RCIA, 459–472). If Reception is scheduled for Easter (a practice that NS 33 prefers parishes to avoid), the Penitential Rite may take place during Mass on the Second Sunday of Lent (RCIA, 462).

The ceremony follows the Liturgy of the Word. After the Scriptures and the homily, the presider invites the community to silent prayer. Intercessions are made for the candidates, and the presider offers a prayer for them, modeled on the scrutinies.

This liturgy has the feel of a Penitential Rite because the candidates are already baptized. In their baptized state they are more responsible for their sinful behavior than unbaptized catechumens are. Consequently, the prayers invite them into a spirit of repentance as they prepare for the Rite of Reception.

65. What is a scrutiny?

A scrutiny is a rite of self-searching and repentance. It intends to uncover and strengthen any weak spiritual resolve in the elect and to bring out and strengthen what is upright, strong, and good. Scrutinies help complete the elect's conversion to Christ (RCIA, 141).

There are three scrutinies. They demonstrate the growing intensity of the season of purification and enlightenment. Through the successive proclamations of the Gospels of the woman at the well (Jn 4:5–42), the man born blind (Jn 9:1–41), and the raising of Lazarus (Jn 11:1–45), the elect come to reject personal sin, spiritual blindness, and the power of death.

A scrutiny includes an exorcism. Formerly this exorcism was addressed to Satan, commanding him to leave the elect. Today the exorcism is addressed to Christ, asking him to drive out the power of evil and to replace it with the Holy Spirit. All the exorcisms are based on this dynamic: out with the bad spirit, in with the good. The exorcism begins with a prayer to the First Person of the Trinity, concludes with a prayer to Jesus, and includes an imposition or extension of hands over the elect for the invocation of the Holy Spirit. The entire Trinity is invoked.

The scrutiny follows a simple structure (RCIA, 150–156, 164–170, 171–177). After the readings and the homily, the presider invites the elect and the assembly to silent prayer. Intercessions for the elect follow. Then the presider pronounces the exorcism. Finally, the elect are dismissed.

In the adaptation for children, the scrutiny is combined with an anointing with the oil of catechumens for unbaptized children and with the first celebration of the Sacrament of Reconciliation for baptized children (RCIA, 291–303). This hybrid could be effective as the communal celebration of first Confession for other children in the catechetical group. Alternatively, children may participate in the scrutinies of the adults. However, only one scrutiny is expected for children. It does not connect to any of the three Gospels that the adult scrutinies accompany, so it may be offered at any time.

66. Why are the Year A Gospels so important for the scrutinies?

The scrutinies are usually celebrated on the Third, Fourth, and Fifth Sundays of Lent. The Scriptures of Year A are to be used in any year at the scrutiny Masses (RCIA, 146).

This practice recaptures a custom from the early Church. From the earliest recorded lectionary, it appears that the Gospels that accompanied the scrutinies were the woman at the well, the man born blind, and the raising of Lazarus. These Gospels, now restored to the aforementioned Sundays of Lent in Year A, are intended to coincide with the scrutinies. Because a parish may have elect in their midst every year, these traditional Gospel passages may be proclaimed any year for the scrutiny Masses.

Some ministers object that in these circumstances the readings of Years B and C for Sundays three, four, and five of Lent may never be proclaimed in a particular parish. This is possible, but the value of the traditional texts is strong, their content is compelling, and the community may well benefit from their annual proclamation. (The readings for other important occasions repeat every year: Christmas, Epiphany, the Assumption, and All Saints, for example.)

In many parishes, the homilist will have different readings at Masses on the same weekend. This suggests two different homilies, as is generally done on weekends when there is a wedding, for example. The homily for the scrutiny Mass may be brief, since the Scriptures and the ritual will themselves speak eloquently about the Paschal Mystery. Or, the Year A readings may be proclaimed at the other Masses that weekend, even if they involve no scrutiny, unifying the preparation for the homily (see the introduction to the Lectionary, 97, which does not limit the usage of these readings to the scrutinies).

67. What is a presentation?

A presentation is a ceremony in which the elect formally receive ancient texts that express the heart of the Church's faith and prayer. They usually take place during the Period of Purification and Enlightenment since they help the final preparation for Baptism (RCIA, 147–149).

These rituals developed over a period of centuries. During the Middle Ages a third presentation was made, that of the four Gospels. In time, the presentations were absorbed into the baptismal rite, but two were revived as independent rituals after the Second Vatican Council. Under some circumstances, the occasion for the presentations may be advanced into the period of the catechumenate. If the pastor and catechumenate team judge that the Period of Purification and Enlightenment seems heavy with ritual, and the period of the catechumenate seems light, or that an earlier reception of these texts would benefit those preparing for Baptism, the presentations may be celebrated prior to the Rite of Election (RCIA, 21, 79, 104–105).

The presentations may be made to baptized but uncatechized candidates (RCIA, 407). However, this should be done only if the candidates have had little or no catechesis (NS, 31). Those who have been catechized and who practiced Christianity in another faith have no need of receiving the Creed, the Lord's Prayer, and the Gospels that have been so much a part of their life. In fact, it could be insulting to offer these rituals to catechized candidates.

68. What is the Presentation of the Creed?

The Presentation of the Creed is the formal handing over of the symbol of Christian faith (RCIA, 157–163). During the ritual, the elect hear the words of the Creed and are invited to make it a part of their life.

The ceremony generally takes place on a weekday during the third week of Lent, after the first scrutiny has been celebrated. It is not to be celebrated during the Sunday Mass, but at another time, preferably when some of the community of the faithful are present.

The service may, but need not, include Mass. After the Scriptures and homily, the faithful who are present recite the Creed for the elect. The presider then leads a prayer over the elect and dismisses them.

Some communities "present" a written form of the Creed to the elect, but this transgresses the origins of the ceremony. The Creed was never written down in the early Church because it was part of the church's teaching kept private for its own members. The Creed was recited by memory with the intent that the elect would then commit it to memory. Even today, the elect are expected to memorize the Creed in the weeks between its presentation and their Baptism (RCIA, 148).

69. What is the Presentation of the Lord's Prayer?

The Presentation of the Lord's Prayer is the occasion when the community formally hands on to the elect the prayer that Jesus taught his disciples. Just as Jesus entrusted this prayer to his faithful followers, so the Church does on this occasion (RCIA, 178–184).

The ceremony is usually held on a weekday during the fifth week of Lent. It is never celebrated during a Sunday Mass, but preferably at another time when some of the community may be present. It may take place during Mass, but need not.

After the first readings, a minister invites forward those who will receive the Lord's Prayer. They approach the ambo. The presider then urges them to be attentive to the reading in which the Lord teaches prayer to his followers. The Gospel is then proclaimed by the presider, even if he is a priest, not by a deacon, because the proclamation of this particular gospel is the presentation, and it belongs to the presider. Alternatively, a deacon may preside for the entire ceremony.

Although some communities "present" a printed version of the Lord's Prayer during the ceremony, the actual presentation comes orally, in the Gospel itself. After the homily the presider leads a prayer over the elect and dismisses them.

70. Should the elect participate in the Triduum?

Yes, catechumens and the elect should participate in the principal services from Holy Thursday through Easter Sunday. Opinions differ, however, on whether or not they should be dismissed.

In general, the elect and catechumens may always be dismissed after the Liturgy of the Word at Mass. There is no special provision for them to remain throughout the liturgy of Holy Thursday. However, in practice, many parishes do invite the unbaptized to remain for the Eucharist that day. These celebrations are so central to Catholic worship that it seems proper to have them experience the Triduum in its fullness. Besides, the entire Triduum resembles one single liturgy. Even though it starts on Holy Thursday night and ends with Easter, there is no dismissal of the assembly at the end of Thursday's Mass of the Lord's Supper nor after Friday's celebration of the Passion of the Lord. People leave, of course, but the liturgy seems suspended, not over. Consequently, one could argue that the elect remain from the beginning of Thursday's celebration through the Easter Eucharist, since no one is dismissed.

A parish may have catechumens who have only recently begun their formation and who will be eligible for Baptism at a future Easter but not this one. In that case, they remain catechumens and do not participate in the Rite of Election or the scrutinies and presentations. Throughout Lent, the elect and catechumens would be dismissed together. Another approach to the Triduum would be to dismiss catechumens but not the elect from the Holy Thursday and Easter services. However, neither group has been baptized, so their ability to participate fully is uniformly limited.

Some parishes utilize catechumens in other ways throughout the Vigil. Some, for example, invite the elect to have their feet washed on Holy Thursday. Nothing in the liturgy promotes or forbids the practice, but the foot washing does not specifically pertain to the elect and may cause more confusion than insight.

71. How important are the preparation rites on Holy Saturday?

The preparation rites are the last ceremonies before Baptism (RCIA, 185–205). They help the elect make their final preparation for initiation. There are no preparation rites for baptized candidates.

The preparation rites are to be celebrated on Holy Saturday morning. At times in the Church's history, these rites were subsumed into the Easter Vigil. However, they stand apart in today's liturgy, permitting catechumens to spend more of the day in prayer and freeing the Easter Vigil to place its focus on Baptism.

The preparation rites include the Ephphetha Rite and the Recitation of the Creed. They may also include the choosing of a baptismal name.

Throughout Holy Saturday the elect should refrain from their usual activities and spend the day in prayer and reflection. They, and all the community, are invited to observe a fast. This fast is not the penitential fast of Good Friday but the fast of preparation for Baptism.

The preparation rites may begin with a song and the greeting of the presider. Scriptures are proclaimed, and a homily follows. The rites themselves come next and the celebration concludes with a prayer of blessing and dismissal.

The bishops of the United States have called the preparation rites "optional" (RCIA, 33.7). These rites may not seem important, but they are preliminary to the celebration of Baptism, which follows later in the day.

72. What is the Ephphetha Rite?

The Ephphetha Rite impresses on the elect their need of grace in order to hear and profess the Word of God (RCIA, 197).

The rite has its origins in a passage from Mark's Gospel (7:31–37), which may serve as a Scripture for this celebration. In the story, Jesus cures a deaf man with a speech impediment by placing his fingers in the man's ears and taking his own spittle to touch the man's tongue. Jesus says the word, "Ephphetha," that is, "Be opened." It is possible that this story inspired prebaptismal vocabulary and gestures in the apostolic Church. The friends who accompany the man seeking a cure even seem to foreshadow godparents.

Throughout the history of Baptism, some version of the Ephphetha Rite has been preserved. Today it ritualizes our desire that the elect receive the word of God in their ears and proclaim it with their lips. Even the illiterate may hear God's Word: The presider does not touch the eyes or fingers of the elect.

When this ceremony is included in the preparation rites of Holy Saturday, it comes immediately after the greeting. The ritual book unfortunately places the texts out of sequence. The Ephphetha Rite appears there after the Recitation of the Creed, but in practice, it should come before. The presider has to untangle the pagination for the rite to flow smoothly.

For pastoral reasons, the Ephphetha Rite may take place during the period of the catechumenate. If the Presentations of the Creed and Lord's Prayer are anticipated, the Ephphetha Rite may conclude these ceremonies (RCIA, 105). A catechumen may actually receive the Ephphetha Rite more than once in this case.

73. What is the Recitation of the Creed?

The Recitation of the Creed prepares the elect for their profession of faith before Baptism (RCIA, 193). It takes place during the preparation rites on Holy Saturday morning.

As the elect received the Creed from the community a few weeks prior, so they now return the Creed to the community. Between these events, they meditate on and memorize the Creed. Their recitation demonstrates their readiness and belief for the community.

Although in many parishes the elect read the Creed from a printed text, ideally they should recite it from memory (RCIA, 148).

If the Ephphetha Rite is included (and it normally is), it should precede the Creed. In this way, after the presider prays that the ears and lips of the elect may be opened, the first words they speak are their faith in the Creed.

If for some reason there was no Presentation of the Creed during the third week of Lent, there should be no Recitation.

In the history of the catechumenate this presentation was called in Latin the *traditio*, and the Recitation of the Creed the *redditio*. This ancient custom was restored in the Church after the Second Vatican Council.

74. Why is there no Recitation of the Lord's Prayer?

Actually, there is a Recitation of the Lord's Prayer. It takes place at the Easter Vigil during the Liturgy of the Eucharist. The elect do not recite the Lord's Prayer until after they have been baptized, when they prepare for Communion together with the assembly of the faithful in the normal course of the Mass.

In our history there exists a tradition for the reciting of the Lord's Prayer prior to Baptism. However, the custom began fairly late and the framers of the restored catechumenate decided to return to the more original custom.

Jesus is the incarnate Son of God. Those who are baptized are adopted children of God. Catechumens may have learned the Lord's Prayer. After their Baptism, however, they claim God as their Father with new meaning for the first time.

If the newly baptized are especially aware of this prayer during the Easter Vigil, it will heighten their preparation for sharing the Eucharist.

75. Should catechumens take a new name at Baptism?

Probably not. The liturgy for the preparation rites on Holy Saturday morning permits the choosing of a baptismal name at that time (RCIA, 200). However, in the United States, the National Conference of Catholic Bishops has established a norm that there is to be no giving of a new name (RCIA, 33.4).

The possibility of giving a new name also appears in the Rite of Acceptance (RCIA, 73). However, it is not recommended in the United States. The option of a new name appears in the Rite of Acceptance because in some cultures other religions impose a new name on those preparing for membership in a parallel ceremony. The possibility appears here so that Christians in such locales would not feel inferior to other religions that encourage the practice.

Not giving a new name has its own significance. The elect will be baptized with their own name, the name people use to address them. So whenever people call a Christian by name, they call the Christian a Christian.

If one of the elect was known by a name that was clearly anti-Christian in its sentiment, she or he could request a new name at this point, in conformity with canon 855. Practically, though, it would make more sense if a legal change in name occurred at the same time.

In most cases, the elect will be baptized with their given name. In place of the ceremony of choosing a baptismal name, during the preparation rites on Holy Saturday the presider could invite the elect to explain how their parents chose their name. That often reveals some of the values that they were intended to inherit.

76. What is the paschal fast?

The paschal fast is part of the spiritual preparation for the Easter Vigil. Those who are to be baptized as well as the faithful are encouraged to abstain from food and drink as much as possible on Holy Saturday (RCIA, 185.1; *Constitution on the Sacred Liturgy*, 110).

The suggestion for keeping a prebaptismal fast dates to the turn of the second century. The practice gave the entire community an opportunity to prepare together for Baptism. Eventually, the prebaptismal fast grew into a fast before Communion, a practice that continues today.

Ash Wednesday and Good Friday are fast days throughout the Catholic world. The fast on those days emphasizes the spirit of repentance that characterizes their celebration. The paschal fast, however, stresses the spiritual preparation one makes for Baptism.

Sometimes we fast from food quite naturally before some big event. We are so excited about the wedding, the exam, the game, the concert, or even the conversation that we just cannot eat. The paschal fast puts our body in the same position. Our anticipation of Baptism and Easter is so great that we fast to heighten its joy.

PART 5:

INITIATION

77. Why does Baptism coincide with Easter?

Baptism coincides with Easter in keeping with an ancient custom in the Church. In the first few centuries there were probably many days on which Baptism was offered, but by the fourth century the practice of baptizing on Easter and Pentecost was becoming much more the norm. Preference for Easter and Pentecost Baptisms has remained in Church documentation ever since. In the liturgy today, Easter is preferred.

This preference exists because of the connection between the events. In the Incarnation, the Word became flesh; Jesus who is God also became human. The rising of Christ from the dead made possible the resurrection of humans. Our Baptism is a first step. It gives us a share in the divine life we will possess perfectly in eternity. When we celebrate Baptism on Easter, our ritual immediately glimpses its goal.

Baptism may take place at other times, especially in cases of emergency. The Baptism of infants is permitted on almost any day of the year. However, Sunday remains the preferred day for infant Baptism because every Sunday is a kind of Easter celebration.

Easter falls each year on the Sunday following the first full moon of spring in the Northern Hemisphere (the hemisphere of Jerusalem). Baptism has cosmic significance. It pertains to the renewal of the universe. We do not baptize adults just when they think they are ready. Not even when their catechists think they are ready. But when the earth is ready. When the sun, the moon, and the stars are ready. When the new Jerusalem is ready. That is when we baptize.

78. Why do we sing the litany of the saints?

We sing the litany of the saints to invoke our ancestors' assistance in the Sacrament of Baptism (RCIA, 221, 570). A litany appeared in the fourth century baptismal liturgy of Jerusalem. It spread more universally in the eighth-century baptismal rites. Because it assigned a short, simple refrain to the assembly, people could sing it while they walked. The litany of the saints became the music that accompanied the procession to the baptismal font.

The litany of the saints at the baptismal liturgy has several parts. It opens with the Kyrie ("Lord, have mercy"). It then proceeds through a list of saints, grouped more or less chronologically as follows: Mary, angels, New Testament figures, martyrs, doctors of the church, founders of religious communities, and women doctors of the church. It concludes with various petitions, including a specific mention of the elect, those chosen for Baptism.

The singing is traditionally led by one or more cantors. The list of saints may include others. The patron of the church, of the city, or of those to be baptized, for example, may be added. These names could be inserted in their proper place in the litany (angels with angels, martyrs with martyrs, etc.). If there is no procession (for example, if the font is in the sanctuary), we still sing the litany.

The adaptation of Baptism for children of catechetical age omits the litany (RCIA, 310). A shorter ceremony will not tax the attention of children as much.

79. Why is water blessed?

We bless water to invoke the assistance of the Holy Spirit in the act of Baptism. We ask the Spirit to come upon the water of the font to make it effective. By the power of the Holy Spirit, the one to be baptized enters water specially prepared for bringing new birth (RCIA, 222, 311, 571).

We bless water in keeping with a tradition dating back to the second century. Those to be baptized removed all clothing and jewelry and entered water purified by prayer, so that they could rise from that water completely reborn, having completely left behind their former way of life. The purification of the water assisted the passage they were making from their former allegiance to life in Christ.

80. Why do the elect make baptismal promises?

The elect make baptismal promises to announce their definitive intention to give their life to Christ (RCIA, 223–225, 313–314, 572–574).

Throughout their formation, catechumens have been preparing to make a conversion, a change of heart. They are leaving behind a life outside the Christian community and entering a life that will find sustenance there. In the Rite of Election they have heard their call to initiation. Throughout the season of purification and enlightenment they have refined their intentions, especially through the celebration of the scrutinies. Now, fortified by the Presentations of the Creed and the Lord's Prayer, and strengthened by the community's prayer, they bring their resolve to its climactic moment. Before they enter the waters of Baptism, they pronounce their faith succinctly and publicly.

In the case of children, the presider may ask parents or guardians, godparents, and all present to recite the Creed before asking the children to profess their faith (RCIA, 312). This obtains the support of the community for the children's young faith.

The presider asks the elect to renounce any allegiance to Satan. If the bishop wishes, additional renunciations may be made here. Is there some other evil that plagues the community or that the elect have repudiated? Violence? Drug addiction? Pornography? Prejudice? Participation in a sect or cult? The elect may publicly renounce these as well. In the United States, however, the renunciations are not normally adapted (RCIA, 33.8). The elect may make the renunciations as a group.

The professions of faith, "Do you believe . . . ?" are best made individually. Each one seeking Baptism expresses her or his belief in the Creed the Christian community holds. The third edition of *The Roman Missal* allows the elect to make their promises at the same time that the entire community renews its baptismal promises (Easter Vigil, 55). But this is the moment in which they declare their faith just before their Baptism. It is more powerful when done individually.

81. How do you baptize somebody?

Baptize by immersing or pouring water over someone while addressing the person by name and reciting the words, "N., I baptize you in the name of the Father, and of the Son, and of the Holy Spirit."

The Catholic Church permits anyone to baptize in an emergency, as long as he or she has the right intention, recites the correct formula, and uses water. In ordinary circumstances a bishop, priest, or deacon baptizes.

The words of the formula of Baptism are of the utmost importance. Everyone should know the words.

In the Catholic Church Baptism may be administered by immersion or by pouring water. Sprinkling is not acceptable. The use of some other liquid besides water is not acceptable.

82. What is Baptism by immersion?

Immersion is always the method listed first and is preferred (RCIA, 226, 317, 575; NS, 17). Immersion has not been possible for many centuries in Catholic parishes because our churches have not been equipped with adequate fonts. Typically, priests baptized infants in a small font that was shared by the few adults. Now, however, the Church urges parishes to prepare adults with a catechumenate and to baptize them in a large enough font. New church buildings often make this provision. Older churches are being retrofitted to accommodate full fonts. Other churches make temporary arrangements; for example, they bring a large container—a plastic pool, a metal stock tank—into the church and decorate it for the Easter Vigil.

For the actual Baptism by immersion, the minister may stand in the water or next to the font, depending on its construction. He may immerse the elect forward or backward, again depending on logistical possibilities. The elect may also kneel in the font while the minister bends them forward, immersing the head. The elect may also stand or kneel in the font while the minister pours water over them.

In the case of infants the minister may hold them, one hand under the child's head and the other under the child's bottom, and gently lower the infant into the font. It is not necessary that water cover the face or head, if parents are concerned. Infants may also sit or be stood up in the font while water is poured over them. In the United States Baptism by immersion is preferred as "the fuller and more expressive sign of the sacrament" (NS, 17). Provision at least for partial immersion—namely, of the candidate's head—should be made.

With regard to clothing, the ritual asks that decorum be observed. There is little cultural resistance to the nudity of an infant for Baptism by immersion. But adults and other children are expected to wear something, contrary to the practice in the early Church where cultural sensibilities permitted the Baptism of naked adults. Those ceremonies were generally conducted in more private areas of the church building, or even outside it. Practically, adults and children of catechetical age may wear into the font whatever they do not mind getting wet. It is not necessary that these clothes be covered with another garment, but many communities promote this practice. In this case, those being baptized wear a simple, loose-fitting garment over their clothes. This garment could be of any color, but preferably not white to avoid confusion with the baptismal garment.

Godparents should have a hand on the elect as they are being baptized. In some fonts, this may be difficult unless they too enter the water. At least, they should receive the newly baptized as they emerge from the font. In the case of infants, the parents' role should predominate.

Baptism also may take place by pouring. In this case the minister can avoid minimizing the symbol by using an abundant quantity of water.

83. Why are the newly baptized not anointed on the crown of the head with chrism right away?

Newly baptized adults are not anointed on the crown of the head with chrism in order to avoid confusion with Confirmation.

When an infant is baptized, the priest or deacon anoints the crown of the child's head with chrism, as Christ was anointed priest, prophet, and king. This ritual first appeared in third- or fourth-century baptismal texts as one of two postbaptismal anointings in the same ceremony: one administered by presbyters outside the church building at the font, the other inside the church building by the bishop. Generally speaking, the first anointing pertained to the ministry of Christ and the second to the outpouring of the Spirit, even though these mysteries are intertwined. For many hundreds of years since, the two anointings were split in the Roman Church for the ceremonies of Baptism and Confirmation. When the Second Vatican Council permitted the presbyter to administer the two sacraments at the Easter Vigil, the double anointing seemed redundant. Consequently, the first is now omitted when Confirmation follows. In the rare instance when someone other than a priest or bishop baptizes at the Easter Vigil—for example, in communities where the unavailability of those ministers causes a deacon to lead a non-Eucharistic Easter service—the deacon does anoint the crown of the head of the newly baptized adult, who will be confirmed at the next opportunity (RCIA, 228, 577). If a catechist or another lay minister baptizes in these circumstances, she or he is not to anoint with chrism because the Catholic tradition reserves sacramental anointings to ordained clergy.

The words "Christ" and "chrism" are related. "Christ" means "anointed one" and "chrism" means a special kind of oil. The word relates to our word "cream."

Only a bishop may consecrate chrism. He does so at the Mass of Chrism, held in the cathedral each year shortly before Easter. Holy Thursday is the traditional day for this Mass, but it may be held earlier for the convenience of those who will be intensely celebrating the Triduum. Chrism traditionally is a mixture of olive oil and balsam, but other oils and perfumes may be used. The bishop blesses two other oils, the oil of catechumens and the oil of the sick, but he mixes perfume only into chrism. Chrism is our most sacred oil. It is used in the Baptism of infants, Confirmation, and priesthood ordination. It is also used for anointing a new altar and the walls of a new church. In general, it accompanies the sacraments and rituals that are done only once in a lifetime, as a sign of the enduring power of the Holy Spirit conferred in those events.

Some have questioned the omission of the postbaptismal anointing with chrism on the crown of the head for adults. Historically it served a separate function from Confirmation. Others believe the postbaptismal anointing for infants should be omitted or assigned the further dignity of Confirmation itself. Although those who framed the current celebration of adult Baptism intended to avoid confusion, they created some confusion with two different anointing sequences.

84. Why do we offer the white garment?

We offer the white garment as a sign that the newly baptized have clothed themselves with Christ (RCIA, 229, 320, 578).

The white garment alludes to several texts of Scripture. In the transfiguration Jesus' clothes became white (Mt 17:2; Mk 9:3; Lk 9:29). In other instances, spiritual beings from heaven wear white vesture: the angels at the resurrection (Mt 28:3; Mk 16:5; Jn 20:12), the mysterious men speaking to the faithful at the ascension (Acts 1:10), as well as the elders before the throne of the lamb (Rev 4:4) and the armies of heaven (Rev 19:14). More importantly, though, the victorious among the faithful (Rev 3:4, 5, 18), martyrs (Rev 6:11), and the throng of those from every nation gathered before the lamb (Rev 7:9, 13, 14) are clothed in white. The text refers to Paul's statements that those in Christ are a new creation (2 Cor 5:17) and are clothed in Christ (Gal 3:27). Thus, when the newly baptized wear a white garment, they assume the clothing of the faithful in heaven, who dress like angels and even like Jesus himself.

The custom originated in the early Church. It helps the newly baptized look forward to eternal life, in which they now have a share. The newly baptized used to wear their garments to daily Eucharist throughout Easter week and again on Pentecost. For this reason we used to call the Sunday after Easter *in albis* (in white) and in some traditions Pentecost has been called "Whitsunday."

Even though the color white is especially fitting for its biblical connotations, the garments may be of another color that conforms to local custom, or the ritual may be omitted (RCIA, 229). The third edition of *The Roman Missal*, however, states that the white garment is given to adults and children (Easter Vigil, 51).

85. Why do we give the newly baptized a lighted candle?

The lighted candle signifies that the newly baptized have been enlightened by Christ (RCIA, 230, 321, 579). We call their immediate preparation for Baptism their Period of Purification and Enlightenment. In some traditions in the early Church the newly baptized were called "the enlightened."

Candles for the newly baptized are lit from the Easter candle. The first lighting of the Easter candle opens the Vigil each year. That light, penetrating the darkness, signifies the Resurrection of Jesus, bringing hope to the world. The faithful who light their candles from the Easter candle shine with the light of Christ and set the church aglow with the fire of faith.

Should those to be baptized hold lighted candles at the beginning of the service? The rubrics are silent on this point. Many believe that the full meaning of the candle is manifest if they do not. Others hold that the light of Christ illumines everyone, even the elect, even nonbelievers.

The Easter candle remains burning throughout Easter Time and for Baptisms and funerals.

In the ritual the celebrant holds the Easter candle while the godparents come forward to light candles from its flame. Godparents present the candles to the newly baptized.

As with the white garment, the candle signifies eternal life. The newly baptized are asked to keep the flame of faith alive in their hearts that they may meet the Lord with all the saints in heaven. The words allude to the parable of the ten bridesmaids (Mt 25:1–13) and Paul's exhortation to live as children of the light (Eph 5:8).

86. What is a neophyte?

A neophyte is someone who is newly baptized. The ritual text generally refers to them as "newly baptized" because the expression is more easily understood. "Neophyte" comes from Greek words meaning "newly planted" or "young sprouts" and can refer to anyone new at something. Neophytes retain their designation throughout the period of mystagogy.

87. Why do we sprinkle the assembly with holy water at the Easter Vigil?

We sprinkle holy water on those already baptized to renew their baptismal commitment. The action follows the spoken renewal of baptismal promises and is coupled with it. The community verbalizes its recommitment to God, then ritualizes it with water from the font. The water for sprinkling is drawn from the font, which was blessed for the Baptisms.

For the faithful this ceremony captures a key moment in the Vigil. The Easter Vigil celebrates the death and Resurrection of Christ, but it is not a mere remembrance of this event. It draws the participant into the same mystery. The early Church made a distinction between Christmas and Easter. Whereas Christmas calls to mind the mystery of the Incarnation, Easter does more than call to mind the mystery of the Resurrection. It pulls believers into participation in the Resurrection— first through the sacraments of initiation for the unbaptized, but also through the spiritual renewal of the baptized. Throughout Lent the faithful have prepared for this renewal. They have observed various disciplines to turn away from sin and recommit themselves to the Gospel. Now they celebrate the new people they have become. All renounce Satan and profess belief in Christ. In this simple action, the community brings to a climax its celebration of Lent.

If there are Baptisms but no Receptions of Baptized Christians into the Full Communion of the Catholic Church, the sprinkling takes place after the Confirmation of the neophytes (RCIA, 237–240). If there are both

Baptisms and Receptions, the sprinkling and the Rite of Reception take place before Confirmation (RCIA, 580–583). This changed the structure of the liturgy as outlined in the 1975 *Sacramentary*, which placed the sprinkling after the Rite of Reception. The change affirms the Baptism of the candidate for Reception. All the baptized are encouraged to renew their promises—including those to be received into the full communion of the Catholic Church. However, the structure gives a less satisfying treatment to Confirmation. By deferring the Confirmation of neophytes until after the Rite of Reception, the close link between their Baptism and Confirmation is loosened. Without the intervening Rite of Reception, the Confirmations appear much more integral to the rite of Baptism.

If children of catechetical age and no other adults are baptized in this ceremony, there is no renewal of baptismal promises and sprinkling of the faithful. The assembly's optional recitation of the Creed (RCIA, 312) apparently takes its place.

In some parishes, in place of sprinkling, the people come to the font to make the sign of the cross or some other gesture with water, just as they do with holy water upon entering the church.

Since sprinkling is not approved as a method of Baptism in the Catholic Church, this ritual will not be confused with Baptism, which takes place by immersion or pouring.

88. What is the Rite of Reception?

The Rite of Reception receives a person baptized in a separate ecclesial community into the full communion of the Catholic Church (RCIA, 473). It generally takes place during Mass and it culminates with Communion.

The rite presumes that those baptized in other ecclesial communities share a common Baptism with Catholics. That Baptism gives them a real, "though imperfect, communion" with us (*Decree on Ecumenism*, 3). That imperfect communion is made full through the Rite of Reception.

Preparation for Reception covers both doctrinal and spiritual matters, but candidates should not be confused with catechumens who are unbaptized. Anything that would equate them "is to be absolutely avoided" (RCIA, 477).

The rite itself is arranged so that "no greater burden than necessary" is required for establishing communion and unity (473). The citation refers to Acts 15:28, which tells of a decision reached by the so-called Council of Jerusalem. At the time, some in the apostolic Church wanted gentiles to become Jews before becoming Christians. But they decided "no greater burden than necessary" should keep them from the Christian community. That spirit pervades the Rite of Reception.

The Reception takes place rather simply. The candidates recite the Creed (or renew their baptismal promises with the community if the ritual takes place at the Easter Vigil). Then they profess their faith in what the Catholic Church "believes, teaches, and proclaims to be revealed by God" (491 and 585). Then the presider pronounces the act of reception, admitting the candidates into full communion (492 and 586). In most cases, Confirmation follows. The presider gives a sign of welcome—clasping hands or embracing, for example. Intercessions are offered. The community may be invited to offer a sign of peace (497). This sign is omitted in the combined rites of initiation and reception (591). Communion, the highlight, follows.

89. What if someone from an Eastern Orthodox Church wishes to become a Catholic?

If the person wishing to be received into the Catholic Church comes from an Eastern Orthodox tradition, the ceremony is different. According to RCIA 474, "no liturgical rite is required." In this case, the person makes a profession of Catholic faith and then shares Communion. Confirmation is omitted because the Catholic Church accepts the sacramentality of all Eastern rite sacraments, including Chrismation. (How all this is done without a liturgical rite is not clarified, but the idea is to do it simply.)

When persons from an Eastern Orthodox Church join the Catholic Church, they join the closest family to their own tradition (*Code of Canons of the Eastern Churches*, 36). For example, a member of the Greek Orthodox Church being received becomes a member of the Greek Catholic Church. Reception into any Catholic Church enables a person to share Communion in a Roman Catholic Church. If a Greek Catholic Church is accessible, the reception more properly takes place there.

If a member of an Eastern Catholic Church wishes to join the Roman Catholic Church, the process becomes more complicated. Petition should be made to the Apostolic Nunciature through the bishops of both churches (*Code of Canons of the Eastern Churches*, 32). Roman Catholics must be careful not to encourage such a transfer of rites. We wish to preserve the manifold Catholic traditions. To try to convince someone to transfer from an Eastern rite into the Roman rite invokes a canonical penalty (*Code of Canons of the Eastern Churches*, 31, 1465).

90. When should the Rite of Reception take place?

The Rite of Reception may take place at any time of the year. Because the sacraments are not to be celebrated on Good Friday or during the day on Holy Saturday, those dates should be avoided. But the Reception of Candidates into the Full Communion of the Catholic Church may take place at any other time. The occasion for Reception is not tied to the liturgical year, but to the candidate's readiness. Just as a parish may offer first Reconciliation, first Communion, and Marriage more than once a year depending on the readiness of those preparing, the same holds for the Rite of Reception. Especially in the case of baptized, catechized candidates, the parish community may offer the Rite of Reception at any time, even after a brief period of formation.

Although the *Rite of Christian Initiation of Adults* makes a strong case for Baptisms at Easter, the case for Receptions at Easter is considerably weaker. In fact, in the United States, the *National Statutes* say, "It is preferable that reception into full communion not take place at the Easter vigil lest there be any confusion of such baptized Christians with the candidates for baptism" (33).

After the publication of the *Rite of Christian Initiation of Adults,* it became common practice in parishes that had both catechumens and candidates in formation to celebrate the combined rites of initiation and reception at the Easter Vigil (562–594). However, passages such as *National Statutes* 33 and 475.2 offer another perspective about the occasion for the Rite of Reception. If the Easter Vigil is to celebrate more fully the meaning of Baptism in the light of the Resurrection, the Rite of Reception belongs more properly to another occasion. To blur neophytes and the newly received will diminish the significance of the very Baptism the Easter Vigil tries to ennoble.

91. When should baptized, uncatechized Catholics receive Confirmation and First Communion?

When the candidates are baptized but uncatechized Roman Catholics (cf. question 11, page 13), the *National Statutes* also advise against celebrating their sacraments at the Easter Vigil (26). To confuse matters, though, the ritual text states that the period of catechesis for these Catholic candidates "should as a rule coincide with Lent" (RCIA, 408) and that the high point "will normally be the Easter Vigil" (409). The occasion for the Confirmation of such candidates depends on the bishop, who is the ordinary minister of that sacrament for those who were baptized Catholics as infants.

Although the RCIA calls this group "candidates", they do not celebrate the Rite of Reception into the Full Communion of the Catholic Church. They are already Catholic by their Baptism as infants.

92. Why is Confirmation part of the Easter Vigil?

Confirmation is part of the Easter Vigil because its conjunction with Baptism "signifies the unity of the paschal mystery, the close link between the mission of the Son, and the outpouring of the Holy Spirit, and the connection between the two sacraments through which the Son and the Holy Spirit come with the Father to those who are baptized" (RCIA, 215).

The full meaning of Confirmation lies not just in its own celebration but also in its close relationship to Baptism. By celebrating the two sacraments together, the Church proclaims the unity of the Paschal Mystery and the mission of the Son and Spirit. This is why adults are not to be baptized at the Vigil unless Confirmation follows immediately, except for serious reasons such as the absence of a bishop or priest.

In the early Church, all adults and infants baptized in the cathedral customarily received an anointing by the bishop. That anointing later came to be called Confirmation. The celebration of Confirmation in conjunction with Baptism stands in concert with the early tradition of the Church and the meaning of Confirmation.

Most Catholics are more familiar with the celebration of Confirmation apart from Baptism. That practice is the norm for those baptized in infancy, under the assumption that Confirmation belongs to the age when the candidate has the use of reason and is able to renew baptismal promises (canon 889.2). However, whenever Baptism occurs according to the *Rite of Christian Initiation of Adults*, there should be no delay in Confirmation.

93. Under what circumstances are priests allowed to confirm?

A priest may confirm when he baptizes "one who is no longer an infant or one already baptized whom he admits into the full communion of the Catholic Church" (canon 883.2). A priest who has this faculty "must use it for those in whose favor the faculty was granted" (canon 885.2). He may also confirm at any Confirmation ceremony with the bishop if the number of persons to be confirmed is large (canon 884). In danger of death, he may confirm any baptized person of any age, including infants (canons 883.3 and 891).

A priest may also confirm a returning apostate. If a person grew up in the Catholic Church, was never confirmed, publicly repudiated Christianity, and then decided to return to the Church, the priest has the faculty to confirm that person when readmitting her or him to the faith. Or, if the person was baptized a Catholic but raised entirely in another religion, the priest has the faculty to confirm that person when readmitting him or her to the faith (NS, 28).

A priest, then, not only may but must confirm any of the elect he baptizes and any baptized candidate he receives into the full communion of the Catholic Church.

94. Must children of catechetical age baptized at the Easter Vigil also be confirmed?

Yes, children of catechetical age, who have prepared for their Baptism through the catechumenate, must be confirmed at the Easter Vigil by the priest who baptizes them.

The Church divides the rites for Baptism between those "for children" and those "for adults." The *Rite of Baptism for Children* pertains to those who are considered infants. The *Rite of Christian Initiation of Adults* pertains to adults and to children of catechetical age (canon 852.1; RCIA, 252). As the titles of these rites reveal, the younger group celebrates Baptism only. The other group celebrates "Christian initiation"—the sacraments of Baptism, Confirmation, and first Communion.

This practice meets resistance from some bishops, priests, and parents. However, the canons of the Church are especially strong on this point. The priest who has the faculty to confirm a child of catechetical age must use it. The reason goes back to the meaning of Confirmation. Confirmation, celebrated with Baptism at the Easter Vigil, expresses the Paschal Mystery. It is not to be omitted except for a serious reason. To separate the two sacraments at the Vigil harms the sacramental expression of the Paschal Mystery. The mission of the Son and the outpouring of the Spirit are intimately related and are celebrated in their unity at the Easter Vigil.

In some regions, children baptized in infancy celebrate Confirmation after their first sharing of Communion. If unbaptized children of catechetical age are baptized in those regions, they should not receive "the sacraments of initiation in any sequence other than that determined in the ritual of Christian initiation" (NS, 19). This causes two different sequences of the sacraments to coexist, as they have throughout most of the history of the Catholic Church.

95. Who should not be confirmed by a priest?

There are several categories of persons who should not be confirmed. For example, a Catholic who is already confirmed cannot be confirmed again. Infants should not be confirmed, except in danger of death.

A baptized but uncatechized Catholic candidate should not be confirmed at the Easter Vigil unless the bishop has given permission. The bishop is always the ordinary minister of Confirmation for a person baptized Catholic as an infant—except in the case of returning apostates (cf. question 93, NS, 28).

A member of an Eastern Orthodox Church who is received into Catholic communion is not to be confirmed since the Catholic Church accepts as valid the Confirmation (Chrismation) this person received at Baptism (*Directory for the Application of Principles and Norms on Ecumenism*, 122). Similarly, we accept the Confirmation of others in schism (e.g., the Polish National Catholic Church).

By contrast, we do not accept the validity of Confirmations from ecclesial communities in the traditions born of the Reformation. Consequently, if Lutherans or Methodists, for example, wish to join the Catholic Church, they will be confirmed during the Rite of Reception, even if they were already confirmed in their own church. The reasons for this concern the meaning of Confirmation and the validity of orders: most other churches do not accept the sacramentality of Confirmation, and the Catholic Church does not officially recognize the ordained ministry of most other communities.

96. How is Confirmation administered?

Confirmation is administered by an imposition of hands and anointing with chrism. If there are no receptions into the full communion of the Catholic Church, Confirmation follows Baptism and takes place at the font. If there are Receptions, both the neophytes and the newly received celebrate Confirmation in the sanctuary. The difference in location is meant to affirm the Baptism of the candidates. Their Confirmation is moved away from the font to more fully distinguish their ceremony from the Baptism they have already received. A song may be sung before the candidates come forward (RCIA, 231, 322, 587).

Once the candidates are assembled, the community prays in silence. The presider then extends his hands over the group and prays for the sevenfold gift of the Holy Spirit (RCIA, 234, 325, 590). Although this part of the ritual bears the heading "Laying on of Hands," the rubric calls for an extension of hands over the whole group at once. An individual imposition of hands, however, would not be foreign to the tradition of Confirmation.

Before the anointing, a minister brings chrism to the presider. As one or both godparents place their right hand on each candidate's shoulder, "the minister of the sacrament dips his right thumb in the chrism and makes the sign of the cross on the forehead of the one to be confirmed." He says, "N., be sealed with the Gift of the Holy Spirit." The newly confirmed responds, "Amen." They exchange words of peace (RCIA, 235, 326, 591).

The ritual book implies that the name to be used at "N." is the baptismal name. It requires no Confirmation name. The practice of administering Confirmation with a new name left the liturgical and canonical books together with the bishop's slap immediately after the Second Vatican Council. Some parishes and dioceses continue this abandoned custom. Because of the significance of the baptismal name, the principal sources explaining the Sacrament of Confirmation (the *Order of Confirmation*, the *Code of Canon Law*, and the *Catechism of the Catholic Church*) no longer urge the choice or use of a Confirmation name.

In some communities, the presider uses oil more abundantly. He may pour oil over the head of the candidate, for example. If so, he should be careful to cross the forehead with oil while reciting the Confirmation formula. Although the rubrics do not specifically call for a sign of peace between the presider and the one being confirmed, an embrace or hand-shake would fittingly accompany their words.

In the adaptation for children, the Confirmation of the newly baptized may be supplemented with the Confirmation of Catholic children who have prepared for the sacrament at the same time (RCIA, 322, 326). If the bishop is not present, he should grant to the priest who presides the faculty to confirm (RCIA, 308).

97. Why is Communion significant at the Easter Vigil?

Communion is the climax of initiation (RCIA, 243). It is the sacramental moment that holds preeminence at the Easter Vigil.

Some of the Fathers of the Church spoke of one's initiation "into the mysteries." That is, Baptism and Confirmation point the way to Eucharist. They cleanse and consecrate the initiate to share worthily the Body and Blood of Christ.

In the adaptation for children, if any Catholic children have been preparing for their first sharing of Communion together with unbaptized companions, they may also receive Communion at this time (RCIA, 308, 329).

98. How is Communion offered to neophytes?

Communion is offered with an admonition. The presider may remind the neophytes of the significance of the Eucharist (RCIA, 243, 329, 594; *The Roman Missal*, Easter Vigil, 64), the center of the whole Christian life. The rubrics say nothing more about this reminder, except to suggest that the presider address a few words to the neophytes about the import of this moment just before "Behold, the Lamb of God."

For example, the presider may include a quotation from St. Augustine's Sermon 272 in his exhortation:

> My brothers and sisters, we come to the moment for which you have longed the most. With joy we share with you our greatest mystery, the body and blood of Christ. 'Be what you see and receive what you are.' Behold, the Lamb of God who takes away the sins of the world.

Communion should be offered under both forms. Perhaps someone could bake fresh bread for the Eucharist (GIRM, 320) and provide a good wine.

PART 6:
MYSTAGOGY

99. What is mystagogy?

Mystagogy is the period of postbaptismal catechesis. Not just the neo-phytes, but members of the entire community grow to deepen their grasp of the Paschal Mystery, meditate on the Gospel, share in the Eucharist, and perform charity (RCIA, 244). Now that the neophytes have experi-enced the rites of initiation, they are in a better position to come to a fuller understanding of them. They can derive a new perception of the Church and the world. Contact with the full community becomes easier and the faithful intensify their own inspiration (RCIA, 244–246).

Precisely understood, the term "mystagogy" refers to catechesis following Baptism. It is a period that pertains to the newly baptized. Those received into the full communion of the Catholic Church may benefit from mystagogy in the sense that the entire community of the faithful does as well. Mystagogy for newly baptized children of catechet-ical age is to be adapted from the adult guidelines (RCIA, 330).

Mystagogy takes different forms. In one sense, mystagogy is a cat-echetical method. It is a way of teaching and understanding. In the early Church, bishops invited neophytes to reflect on the symbols of initiation and to compare them with similar images in their lived experience, to gain a better understanding of the religious symbol. For example, they could reflect on the process of making bread or the role of water in their lives. Then as they realized that many grains become one loaf, that water provides the source of life, they deepened their appreciation of the sac-ramental mysteries they experienced. In the early Church, mystagogy accomplished this kind of catechesis.

Several liturgical rites identify this period as well. Sunday Masses of the Easter season are called "Masses for neophytes." They and their godparents should attend. The instructions they receive will form the entire community as well (RCIA, 248). During the octave of Easter the prayers at Mass assume that the neophytes are present every day. The period of mystagogy concludes with some celebration near Pentecost (RCIA, 249). However, the US bishops encourage groups to meet monthly for a year (NS, 24). The bishop is encouraged to celebrate a Mass for neophytes sometime during the year (RCIA, 251). The anniversary of their Baptism should also be marked with some celebration in which they may renew their commitment (RCIA, 250). Formerly, the Church provided Mass texts for such a celebration, but the current Missal no longer includes them.

Mystagogy, then, is a blend of liturgy and catechesis following the celebration of initiation.

100. What does a mystagogy session look like?

There is no universal agreement on the answer to this question. This implies that the primary mystagogic catechesis takes place during the Sunday Mass. While the community is assembled, the faithful and the neophytes receive instruction on the sacraments and the Paschal Mystery, presumably during the homily.

However, separate catechetical sessions may take place. A catechist may engage the neophytes in a reflection on the symbols of the Easter Vigil. A beautiful, nourishing celebration of that liturgy will make this easier. If the symbols are clearly and abundantly used (e.g., Baptism by immersion, an aromatic chrism, Communion under both forms), mystagogy can be more fruitful.

Some communities use this time to "get the neophytes involved." They invite representatives of different parish organizations to explain their work or ministry to the newcomers. Well intentioned as this is, mystagogy is not really the time to recruit volunteers. It is a time to deepen our understanding of the Paschal Mystery. Besides, service to the Church and community should have been part of the neophytes' lives long before Baptism, during the period of the catechumenate (RCIA, 75.4).

101. Why is the Easter octave significant for neophytes?

The Easter octave is significant for neophytes because it extends the celebration of Easter. As each day proclaims that Jesus is risen from the dead, so each day announces Baptism's promise of eternal life. The significance of Easter is so big it takes eight days to proclaim it.

The Masses of the Easter octave do this in many ways. About half the presidential prayers (the Collect, the Prayer over the Offerings, and the Prayer after Communion) that week refer to Easter's Baptisms. The Gloria is sung or recited every day, just as on Easter. The Easter Sequence may be sung or recited every day, just as on Easter. The Gospel each day proclaims one account of the Resurrection. The first preface of Easter permits the insertion "on this day"—not just "in this time." Inserts to the first Eucharistic Prayer do the same and mention those newborn in Baptism as if they are present. The Mass closes with a double alleluia, as on Easter day. In short, every day is Easter. Many of these texts and traditions derive from a period in the Church when the newly baptized came to Mass every day during the week after Easter, dressed in their white robes. The *Rite of Christian Initiation of Adults*, however, does not make the same recommendation. If neophytes attended these Masses, they could celebrate the joy of the Eucharist over a more extended period, and their presence would add dramatically to the community's proclamation of Easter's Good News.

102. Why is Year A so important in mystagogy?

According to the *Rite of Christian Initiation of Adults*, 247, the readings for lectionary Year A are especially fitting for the Masses for neophytes. They may be used every year.

The reason, though, is not at all clear. There is no long tradition behind these Scriptures as there is for those of the scrutiny Masses (which may also use the Year A readings every year). The Easter Scriptures for Years B and C seem equally compelling. Admittedly, the second reading during the Easter season of Year A, from the First Letter of Peter, abounds in baptismal imagery. Perhaps the passages from Acts and John's Gospel, which round out the Easter Scriptures of Year A, are more foundational than those in B and C. Otherwise the particular genius of Year A for mystagogy remains hidden.

103. How do you keep neophytes in mystagogy?

One of the most troubling parts of catechumenate ministry is that neophytes do not stick around much for mystagogy. The problem seems nearly universal.

Various explanations may be offered. After learning that initiation will culminate at Easter, many assume that they have "graduated" from formation and no longer attend gatherings. Sessions that nourish can also deplete energy, and neophytes may need a break. The team may need one too. Perhaps the celebration of the Vigil lacked engagement, and there seemed little to discover from reflecting on it. The neophytes may have learned about Baptism and the Eucharist as part of their prebaptismal formation and sense no urgent need to contemplate these mysteries again. Or perhaps their integration into the community feels successful and they do not perceive the need for separate sessions any more.

In addition, more than any other part of the entire *Rite of Christian Initiation of Adults*, the circumstances surrounding mystagogy today are enormously different from those in the early Church. At that time, the initiation rites were kept secret from catechumens and the elect. Only during their initiation did they contact the symbols of water, bread, and wine for the first time. During their formation, they were dismissed from the liturgy quite regularly after the word service, and the faithful did not openly discuss their Creed nor the Eucharist. For this reason, after the neophytes experienced the fertile symbols of initiation, they needed some time to talk about what they heard, touched, and tasted. Out of this raw material came a prolific mystagogic catechesis. The need for mystagogy was directly related to the secrecy that enshrouded Christian ritual. Today, that secrecy is gone, and no one wants it back. Furthermore, catechists, pastors, and bishops want those in formation to know about the Catholic sacraments before initiation, so catechesis on these matters precedes Baptism, whereas it followed Baptism in the early Church. And, in a culture as celebrity-conscious as ours, we should not overlook the role of the catechist. The customary catechist for mystagogy in the early Church was none other than the bishop. No offense to our fine catechists today, but they cannot compete with that kind of star power.

When the framers of the catechumenate restored mystagogy, they did not take these historical factors into account.

To keep neophytes in mystagogy, you will have to convince them long before Easter that more work follows afterward. You will need an Easter celebration that cries out for discussion when it concludes. You will have to provide sessions so compelling in their inspiration that neophytes will be anxious to come.

But the solution may be simpler. You provide good preaching and a good Sunday liturgy so that the neophyte Masses accomplish the mystagogic catechesis they should have. On another occasion or two, you invite neophytes to share their experiences of the sacraments and of life as a Catholic. You shape their insights. That may be enough.

104. Why is there a bishop's Mass for neophytes?

The bishop's Mass for neophytes takes place so that the bishop may have personal contact with the newly baptized (RCIA, 251).

The bishop, after all, directs the ministry of Baptism for the diocese (General Introduction, 12). In an ideal world, he would baptize all his elect and personally welcome them to the Body of Christ. Practically, this is difficult because of the large numbers of those to be baptized and the distances involved. Besides, parish communities exercise the bishop's ministry in local settings. Baptism makes sense as part of the local church's annual Easter celebration.

To compensate for the impossibility of the bishop baptizing so many, the *Rite of Christian Initiation of Adults* makes two accommodations. It recommends that the Rite of Election be held in the cathedral, and it promotes a neophyte Mass with the bishop. Historically, the Rite of Election was no more a cathedral liturgy than the Rites of Acceptance or scrutinies or Baptism. Theologically, if the bishop could be present for only one liturgy, it should be Baptism. Instead, catechumens now come to him to be named among the elect. And they are invited to return after Baptism to celebrate Eucharist with the spiritual father of their diocese.

105. What kind of anniversary celebration of Baptism should there be?

The nature of the anniversary celebration is up to the local church (RCIA, 250). The ritual recommends that those baptized the previous year come together to thank God, to share their experiences, and to renew their commitment. The format envisions a combination of prayer and spiritual sharing. Perhaps it could appear among a parish's offerings the next Lent or be celebrated in connection with one of the following year's neophyte Masses.

106. Should the newly baptized prepare for the Sacrament of Reconciliation?

It would be a good idea. Many are actually hungering for their first Confession. Although Confession is only obligatory for those in mortal sin, it is beneficial for every Catholic. The team could help the neophytes arrange a time for Confession. Godparents could help them prepare.

107. What kind of pastoral care do we offer after mystagogy?

After mystagogy the neophytes receive the same pastoral care as the faithful. But a good pastoral team will keep an eye on the new sheep of the flock. They will help them make their commitment firm. It may be good to visit with neophytes from time to time to ask how their experience is going, whether being a Catholic is what they were expecting, whether they are exhilarated or disappointed by the experience, what challenges they face as a Catholic, and what spiritual insights they have received.

The Spirit of God is alive and well in the Church, especially in the hearts of neophytes. Conversation with them will fortify the Body of Christ. Together with them we will shoulder the gentle yoke of the One whose mission we share, whose life we live, and in whose promise we believe.

Bibliography

Code of Canon Law. Washington, DC: Canon Law Society
of America, 1983.

Code of Canons of the Eastern Churches. Washington, DC: Canon Law
Society of America, 1992.

Congregation for the Clergy. *General Directory for Catechesis*.
Washington, DC: United States Catholic Conference, 1997.

Harmless, William. *Augustine and the Catechumenate*. Rev. ed.
Collegeville: Liturgical Press, 2014.

Johnson, Maxwell. *The Rites of Christian Initiation: Their Evolution
and Interpretation*. Rev. ed. Collegeville: Liturgical Press, 2007.

Morris, Thomas H. *The RCIA: Transforming the Church*. Rev. ed.
Mahwah: Paulist Press, 1997.

Pontifical Council for Promoting Christian Unity. *Directory for
the Application of Principles and Norms on Ecumenism*.
Vatican City, 1993.

Rite of Christian Initiation of Adults. International Commission
on English in the Liturgy and Bishops' Committee on the
Liturgy. Chicago: Liturgy Training Publications, 1988.

Rito de la iniciación cristiana de adultos. International Commission
on English in the Liturgy and Bishops' Committee on the
Liturgy. Washington, DC: United States Conference of
Catholic Bishops, 2008.

Satterlee, Craig A., and Ruth Lester. *Creative Preaching on the
Sacraments*. Nashville: Discipleship Resources, 2001.

Steffen, Donna. *Discerning Disciples: Listening for God's Voice in Christian Initiation.* 2nd ed. rev. Chicago: Liturgy Training Publications, 2018.

Turner, Paul. *Ages of Initiation The First Two Christian Millennia.* Collegeville: Liturgical Press, 2000.

———. *Celebrating Initiation: A Guide for Priests.* Franklin Park: World Library Publications, 2007.

———. *When Other Christians Become Catholic.* Collegeville: Liturgical Press, 2007.

Vatican Council II. *Decree on Ecumenism.* Vatican City: 1964.

Yarnold, Edward. *The Awe-Inspiring Rites of Initiation: The Origins of the RCIA.* 2nd ed. Collegeville: Liturgical Press, 1994.

Recommended Reading

Birmingham, Mary. *Year-Round Catechumenate*. Chicago: Liturgy Training Publications, 2003.

Burns Senseman, Rita. *Guide to Adapting the RCIA for Children*. Chicago: Liturgy Training Publications, 2017.

Huels, John M. *The Catechumenate and the Law: A Pastoral and Canonical Commentary for the Church in the United States*. Chicago: Liturgy Training Publications, 2003.

Lewinski, Ronald J. *An Introduction to the RCIA: The Vision of Christian Initiation*. Chicago: Liturgy Training Publications, 2017.

Paprocki, Joe, and D. Todd Williamson. *Great is the Mystery: Encountering the Formational Power of Liturgy*. Chicago: Liturgy Training Publications, 2013.

Regan, David. *Experience the Mystery: Pastoral Possibilities for Christian Mystagogy*. Collegeville: Liturgical Press, 1994.

Ruzicki, Michael. *Guide for Training Initiation Ministers: An Introduction to the RCIA*. Chicago: Liturgy Training Publications, 2018.

Tufano, Victoria M., Paul Turner, and D. Todd Williamson. *Guide for Celebrating Christian Initiation with Adults*. Chicago: Liturgy Training Publications, 2017.

Turner, Paul. *Hallelujah Highway A History of the Catechumenate*. Chicago: Liturgy Training Publications, 2000.

Wilbricht, Stephen S. *The Role of the Priest in Christian Initiation*. Chicago: Liturgy Training Publications, 2017.

Resources for Group Reflection and Learning

Anslinger, Leisa, Mary A. Ehle, Biagio Mazza, and Victoria M. Tufano. *The Living Word: Leading RCIA Dismissals, Year A.* Chicago: Liturgy Training Publications, 2019.

———. *The Living Word: Leading RCIA Dismissals, Year B.* Chicago: Liturgy Training Publications, 2017.

———. *The Living Word: Leading RCIA Dismissals, Year C.* Chicago: Liturgy Training Publications. 2018.

Egan, Keith. *Words of Faith: Our Prayers.* Notre Dame: Ave Maria Press, 2009.

Gawrych, Andrew. *Words of Faith: Spiritual Practices.* Notre Dame: Ave Maria Press, 2013.

Gensler, Gael, osf, Timothy A. Johnston, Corrina Laughlin, and Kyle Lechtenberg. *Disciples Making Disciples: Print and Digital Resources for Forming the Assembly.* Chicago: Liturgy Training Publications, 2017.

Seeing the Word: The Baptism of Jesus. Collegeville: Liturgical Press, 2011.

Seeing the Word: The Crucifixion. Collegeville: Liturgical Press, 2011.

Seeing the Word: Raising of Lazarus. Collegeville: Liturgical Press, 2010.

Seeing the Word: The Resurrection. Collegeville: Liturgical Press, 2011.

Seeing the Word: The Transfiguration. Collegeville: Liturgical Press, 2010.

About the Cover Art

Christian initiation is a "gradual process that takes place within the community of the faithful" (*Rite of Christian Initiation of Adults*, 4). It is a spiritual journey of catechesis, prayer, and life within the Christian community, leading participants to conversion and enlightenment as they come to know Jesus Christ. This journey normally culminates by celebrating their Baptism, Confirmation, and Eucharist at the Easter Vigil. Through this initiation, they are united with Christ and become members of his mystical Body, the Church.

Cody F. Miller's art depicts the three Gospels proclaimed when the scrutinies are celebrated. These rites are celebrated during the Period of Purification and Enlightenment. The images of the woman at the well, the man born blind, and the raising of Lazarus recall the victory over sin and death that is brought about by Baptism into Jesus Christ, who is the living water, the light of the world, and the source of eternal life.

About the Artist

Mr. Miller was born in Columbus, Ohio, and resides there with his wife and two sons. He received his BFA in 1995 from the Columbus College of Art and Design in Columbus. Mr. Miller is currently a resident artist at the Goodwill Art Studio and Gallery.

He works with cut paper and paint "to convey some degree of hope . . . in a way which shows the quiet fingerprint of God saying, 'I was here all along.'" You can view his work at www.codyfmiller.com.